BECOMING BELOVEDS

becoming beloveds

A PRACTICAL GUIDE

TO BUILDING

STRONGER RELATIONSHIPS

Kari Henley & Steven Cardinale

Library of Congress Cataloging-in-Publication Data

ISBN 978-1-7345010-0-1

DEDICATION

To Chip Conley, for drawing us like fireflies to your Baja shores, and forever altering the trajectory of our lives.

To Saul Kuperstein for your spiritual wisdom inspired by the whispers of a century-old cactus named Alfredo.

To all of us who aspire to strive for something greater, to take risks and to believe in the unending and ever-evolving power of Love.

ACKNOWLEDGMENTS

We wish to express our deepest gratitude to HB who, like a mindful muse, gave form to this book with all her skill, insights and dedication.

Thank you to dear friends who helped us to discover, sort, and create our own Song of Songs.

And we would like to thank our children and family for your love and unique presence in this world. You are our hearts.

TABLE OF CONTENTS

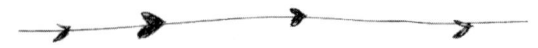

WHAT IS A BELOVED?

Beloved is a vastly potent yet misunderstood word. We know it is about love, but have you ever used the word directly? Perhaps it conjures the image of a minister spreading his hands and intoning, *"Dearly beloved, we are gathered here today,"* when officiating a wedding ceremony. Others think of the iconic book by the late Toni Morrison.

Yet how many couples do you know who call one another beloved?

My Beloved.

The words roll around your tongue like shimmering melted chocolate. Imagine referring to your partner as beloved instead of honey or sweetheart. It is deeper, more potent, even a bit erotic. What if someone called *you* beloved in moments of tenderness, or when introducing you, instead of wife, husband, boyfriend or girlfriend?

There is something about it that is, well, magical. Mystical. Transcendent. It is something we say in hushed tones and represents a quality most of us never imagine having in our everyday relationships. There is an energy about it. Think of the word beloved as a master teacher sending you on a journey to explore a higher and more conscious dimension of love.

Do you have a beloved? Are you being the kind of partner that would merit being called a beloved?

There is a puzzle hidden in the word. It belies far more than conveyed at first glance. Beloved contains both a directive *and* a practice.

First the directive: *BE* love.

Then comes the practice: Be LO*VED*.

It all starts with you. Fall in love with the power of love. Commit yourself to BE love. Love encompasses many things. Say "yes" to them all. Say "yes" to Love for yourself, to a magnificent someone in your life, and say "yes" to a new paradigm or vibration more refined and clearer than you imagined possible.

If you do the work and elevate yourself to this level, you can begin the practice: be LOVED. This requires courage, vulnerability and openness. Allow yourself to be loved, truly adored by those around you.

This may seem like the easier side of the beloved puzzle, but it is not. In order to allow ourselves to be loved, we must open up. We must become fluid with the future as we release the past. We must let go of self-judgment.

None of us have arrived here without our share of wounds, heartaches and regrettable moments. Yet, if we hide our true selves away and push our hearts into a dark closet, we will never fully understand that it is possible to be seen, understood and cherished for exactly who we are.

We have been taught to surround ourselves with shame. We have been taught that sarcasm and poking at people's faults is acceptable. Unconsciously we sabotage little moments and gestures of love because we don't think we deserve it.

When someone shows you love, a choice arrives. You can receive it and Be Loved, or you can shut down.

You can allow yourself to be lifted by that gift, or refuse the exchange.

Be LOVED.

When we rebuke a gesture of love by ignoring it, or by deliberately offering a negative response; it generates separation, rejection, loneliness and pain. Receiving is vulnerability, and requires being present and taking in love as a gift. Nothing else is required.

Allowing ourselves to be loved means we are worthy of being paid attention to. Being loved gives us courage. It changes our perspectives and makes everything possible. Because it is.

Falling in love is the equivalent of being given a sacred fire to hold in your hands. Often, we waste it, ignore it, push it away, sabotage, or refuse to surrender into it. Don't do that. Let it be an alchemical fire instead. Let love lead you wherever it wants you to go.

BE love.

Be *LOVED*.

Your task is not to seek love, but merely to seek and find all the barriers within yourself you have built against it.
- Rumi

This recognition was the beginning of our journey to higher love. One that required a lot of growth, surrender, trust and witnessing to even begin to understand.

The journey is not easy, but it is so worth it. It is everything. When you are finally able to rise through the barriers built and recognize a beloved in your life, nothing will ever be the same. We did it, so can you.

This book was written to reflect our experience of becoming students of higher love. It felt like a directive. Words just came through. Ideas poured out, and lots of original poems seemed to write themselves. Poetry is a wonderful exercise to capture a special moment or elevated emotion that simple sentences or phrases cannot possibly reach. We have featured a couple of our original poems in this book. Indeed, poetry became one of our wise teachers on this journey.

The following original poem was written early one morning while on a glorious bike ride. The poem told of our hero's journey; and became a guiding light. In turn, as this book began to take shape, it became clear that the stanzas reflected the sequential steps required for a journey to understand love's highest teaching. Hence each of the subsequent chapters in this book reflect one of the poem's stanzas and will guide you on your way.

Beloved Love

That's all there is
And all there ever will be
The entrance and the path.
Earn Love
Create Love
Build Love
Nurture Love
Elevate Love
Reflect Love
Expand Love
Declare Love
BE Love
Be LOVED
Become a beloved to another
Allow another to become your beloved
Let's Begin.

INTRODUCTION

WELCOME TO THE JOURNEY OF
BECOMING BELOVEDS

We are so glad you are here. Pull up a chair, get cozy and stay awhile. We are here to ponder and prepare for love. Why are we all so fascinated by it? We long for and are inspired by extraordinary love in action. We have been contemplating love throughout the ages. The centuries-old poems of Rumi, Homer and Sappho are still potent and relevant today. The *Song of Songs*, written almost seven thousand years ago, could still serve as lyrics for so many modern love songs.

Close your eyes for a moment and think back to the first time you identified that feeling of falling in love. Your heart was pounding, excitement coursing through your veins; you felt like you had boundless energy and could conquer the world, or at least do a backflip. What if we could have that enchantment on an ongoing basis, even after the initial head-over-heels?

There are very few resources to help couples sustain that magic, to remain alert to the growth potential of love. There are scores of online dating options to help you find a mate. Yet, what comes after you graduate from the dating site and before you go to couples therapy? Where is the continuing education for love?

The last real education most of us had about relationships and sex was in high school. Today most of us are running around with the same old playbook we learned from other clueless adolescents. We have not been taught how to be good lovers or decent partners to one another. Vision and trajectory for lasting love is not aspired to or understood. We just slip rings on each other's fingers, kiss, and hope for the best.

We enter significant and serious relationships with little support or direction to keep them playful, connected and growing. Work, bills, family and friends pull us in every direction. With all of the outside pressures fraying our relationships, love often becomes like a comfortable but neglected piece of furniture. We could make the effort to rearrange it or reupholster or get new pillows, but it's functional for now so we put it off.

We can't keep putting it off. We need to look now for guidance on what to do after and beyond and in between the big ceremonial moments. There are plenty of articles, books and workshops offering support for when couples hit a rough patch or are in crisis. Essentially there's a huge industry exploring the negative side of love, the not-so-happily-ever-after.

What about the celebratory side? There is a lot of literature on the positive side of love as well, but it is more the stuff of fairy tales, romance novels and greeting cards. While pretty and romantic, it doesn't identify what needs to be done routinely to nurture a significant relationship that is positive, conscious, playful and ever-growing.

Between the fairy tale and the couples therapy; that is the gorgeous messy neglected middle where we want to play and learn. The majority of our loving relationships require practical tools to manage the boring and brittle stuff, and sometimes we need rituals, poetry and play to lift our spirits.

That is why we wrote this book, to inspire individual self-reflection and to elevate the uninspiring or conflicted aspects of relationship to a revitalized romance. To develop a practice for individuals and couples to attend to the greater side of love's potential. We deconstructed the experiences we've had that brought us here to our own enchanted relationship, and we want to share what we've learned with you.

We are all on a journey to explore what love means in our lives, to reignite our imagination, and to find tools to craft a new world for our hearts. We need new habits to care for ourselves and for our partners in a way that is nourishing and interdependent. Rather than visiting a therapist's office to discuss what is wrong, we want you to read this book and learn to celebrate what is right in your relationship. We hope that you will dedicate time, energy and desire towards rising to your highest potential as a couple.

It starts with just one wonderfully simple word: Beloved.

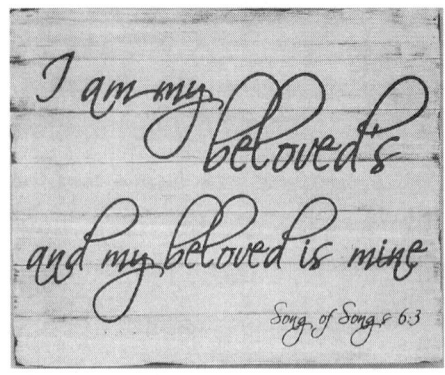

I am my beloved's and my beloved is mine
Song of Songs 6:3

This is a powerful and celebrated phrase from the *Song of Songs*, one of the most beautiful love poems ever written, found in the Old Testament scrolls from the 10th century BC. The verses are an exchange between a man and a woman describing the mutual excellence and supremacy of their beloved in courtship and marriage. There are many academic and religious interpretations, but the one we like the most is that the songs celebrate the joy and goodness of love and the fulfillment and harmony that come with it. For us, this ancient term is so potent. It articulates the modern future of love.

Let the word beloved serve as a guide as you explore this book. It is a powerful journey; following your bliss first into yourself and then with a partner. The pages you have in your hands are lyrical to read and will offer a new mindset with playful romantic tools to build a more conscious, connected relationship. Join the movement. Become students of higher love.

Personal + Relationship Development = Us 2.0

Personal development is something many of us turn to at some point in our lives. We understand that it takes both investment and effort to get in shape, eat healthier foods, or build a focus to achieve success.

What about relationship development? Is there such a section at the bookstore? Nope. Is there a shelf of volumes describing how to maximize relationship potential? How about couple's empowerment? Surely there are tons of resources out there for that category. Umm, nada.

Most of the books and resources, while helpful and useful, are essentially written for struggling couples trying to cope in times of trouble. They are for those attempting to figure out how to reconnect, or maybe deciding whether to stay or go.

Academics and experts write relationship books filled with models, theories and suggestions from the laboratory or lectern. But love doesn't want that. Love wants to be inspired. Relationships thrive on romance and sweetness. Love thrives on stories, journeys and adventures.

Love is good for you. Being happy and secure in love will improve your health and lengthen your life. When we are beloved we sleep better, eat better, feel more engaged in our outer world, and experience more moments of inner awe, gratitude and flow in life.

Rising up to be your best self for your partner is a wonderful motivator. Learning and growing individually and then within your relationship is extraordinary. Couple's improvement fosters the best kind of self-improvement. And vice-versa.

If you boost your relationship and invest in its growth, you will be a better person individually. If you continue to grow within yourself, it follows that your relationship will benefit. A beloved relationship is a crafted conscious love that inspires growth inside and out. The new equation: Me + You = Us 2.0.

So many couples begin their relationship with enchantment, rapture, and colorful passion. For a time, it is so good. For a time, it seems like the honeymoon will never end; until it does. And then we don't know what to do. We invest in this house of love and barely step through the door before we find ourselves reclining in the La-Z-Boy chair of disconnection and complacency.

Maybe we just become apathetic and forget to tell our partners that they are the most gorgeous creature to ever scramble an egg. Maybe we don't want to stop being quietly mad at the world. Could be we are scared to be vulnerable. Or maybe we just haven't been taught that love can and does build over time.

We all want to be in love in a way that takes our breath away. We all want to find someone who we can't stop thinking about no matter if it is year one, twenty-one or sixty-one. We want the honeymoon to last for more than a few months: we want to go beyond the happily-ever-after.

Maybe those honeymoon moments are still there, we just don't awaken them anymore. They require a sweet simple kiss out of nowhere, a special look, or a surprise evening of candles and romance. Love must be nurtured and held as an ongoing priority. Hormones alone will not carry you down the finish line to being a happy couple long term. Infusing honeymoon moments into every day is the key.

If you have picked up this book then you have an intuition that there is something deeper and more magical out there for your relationship. There is.

The most desired gift of love is not diamonds or roses or chocolate. It is focused attention.
- Rick Warren

Achieving blissful love is not a passive accident. Becoming Beloveds requires you to pay attention. It requires each partner to earn it over and over again. And you better believe it takes courage, patience, presence, responsibility, and creativity.

Learning how to pay attention and savor moments with your partner is the point. No matter if you are resetting your standards for the next relationship, just dating, newly together or decades on, there is always room to expand your romantic universe.

Not only do you have to find the right person, you have to become the right person, and you also have to decide to build the right relationship. Becoming Beloveds is a pathway to be earned, and a gift to be savored. We did a lot of research, condensed scores of books, cherry-picked some of the best learning we could find, and infused it with our own thoughts, stories, and reflections to offer something different.

Think of this book as a relationship retreat, a romantic spa day, or routine ritual. Our gift to you.

Our favorite motto on which we base most of our choices is: "You can have any life and any love you want. All you have to do is decide". Our introduction closes with another original poem, our own *Song of Songs*. Perhaps the word beloved will evoke a poem in you too.

What is a Beloved?

A beloved stirs something
You didn't know was there.
A beloved awakens
Aspects of yourself
Carefully tucked away
A beloved reveals
Potential.
Nudges you to be seen
Fully, as you are
A beloved is attentive
In sweet & gentle ways
A beloved knows when
To hold space
And when to come closer
A beloved is a treasure you marvel
At discovering

CHAPTER 1

EARN LOVE ~ THE DOORWAY

The more you love, the more loving you become. That's just the way it works. It is a generosity of spirit.
- Jean Houston

We are sending you on a journey, an expedition into yourself and into your understanding of love. Imagine that you are about to open a door and begin this magnificent voyage. This quest is both for your inner reflection and for couple reflection, but begin the adventure for yourself. Let it blossom in you first and then let your partner become intrigued.

This journey is a sequential and specific process that begins with earning love. There are several stops along your way requiring you to pause, engage, reflect and learn. It is designed to peak your curiosity with enticing new ideas, engage your senses with imagery, and lift your spirits with metaphor and poetry. It is not a passive experience. Oh no. We want you to get your fingers dirty, your cheeks flushed, and your toes wet. We will offer reflections, journal prompts and honeyed new habits to drizzle onto your partner in sweet little ways.

Everything about this journey revolves around the power of intention. There is great potency in earning something. It creates agency and commitment. It implies digging in, not getting it right the first time, and sticking with it.

Creating an intention is how we begin the process to earn something important. It is like placing an order at a restaurant with the Universe as chef. If you don't know what you want, the Universe cannot bring it to you. If, however, you place a very precise intention as your order, you are much more likely to receive exactly what you want.

In her SuperSoul podcast, power manifestor Oprah Winfrey discussed intention with the spiritual teacher Gary Zukav.

Oprah: "The Principle I use to rule my company, and the principle I use for every action in my life, is Intention. It is the heart of creating authentic power.

Zukav: Intention is a quality of consciousness that you bring to a deed or words. It is an energy. It is your reason, and your motivation."

There is an intention behind why you are reading this book right now. Think about the possible energies, reasons and motivations around your relationship. For most of us, the state of relationship falls into one of the following categories with the related intentions:

- **Good to Great** - You're in a relationship that is lovely. It is warm, comfortable and sweet. It's good. You would love to find some special gems to indulge, share, and celebrate. Your intention is to learn and grow.

- **What Happened?** - This usually comes after a relationship that ended badly. You are trying to figure out what went wrong, to diagnose and understand. Your intention is to figure out what did I miss?

- **Starting Over** - Whether you are in a new relationship or just thinking about one, you are starting from scratch. You are trying to get a handle on where the red flags might be hiding. Your intention is to ensure that you don't repeat past mistakes.

- **Grasping** - Sometimes love loses its way. You know something is not right, and don't know what to do. Your intention is to get your relationship back on the right path.

Whether you see yourself in one of these examples, or something unique bubbles up in you, the clarity of your intention will be the factor that transforms this book from a fun read to a game changer. Write it down. Just jot your intention down right now in the margin of the page. Focus on that word or phrase as you begin your journey.

Imagine standing in front of a beckoning doorway. Through a glowing peephole, you can see a landscape filled with magical scenery and sparkling possibility. The door is a portal to another world. It is beckoning you to grab the handle, swing it wide, and step through.

Have you ever felt that vague uneasy sense of knowing your life is about to change? Those moments of wondering, "is this all there is" in life or relationship? Perhaps it is the universe nudging you to notice that door over there.

This is where we must begin: with you. In order to become a student of higher love, you have to decide it is time to step through the doorway and find out what is on the other side. Once you do, make a commitment to do whatever it takes to show up and step up. Whether that means having the courage to leave a relationship, or the courage to fully commit to one. The soul knows, and will continue to send you messages, signals and sometimes uncomfortable sensations to pull you through the doorway and embrace the next chapter of your life.

It is all about earning it. The work you do to earn the life you intend to live is the key. It will open every door you confront. Some think of it as saying, "Yes" to every opportunity that comes your way. That is your intention.

It can be utterly terrifying to step through the door. What does it take for that one final nudge? Think about transitions in the past that are now comfortably in the rear-view mirror.

Reflection
Think about a situation in which you were inspired by something beyond yourself, and made a powerful decision. What was it?

In the book *Eat, Pray, Love,* the writer Elizabeth Gilbert shared her example of saying yes to the wild and sometimes terrifying impulses of life, and earning an entirely new world. She opened her story feeling numb, depleted and worn out from her marriage. She wanted to earn a higher version of herself, and to find new intention. She created a massive doorway of grand adventure, living three months each in Italy, India and Bali. Stepping across the threshold of fear, uncertainty and utter surrender, she came to know herself.

The process of earning it typically begins with a simple decision. Maybe it happens like a thunderbolt as it did for Gilbert, or maybe it is a revelatory moment in a therapist's office, or perhaps it comes in a dream. Maybe it will happen right now as you read these pages.

Are you ready to let go of old habits or patterns that are holding you back and say yes to the beckoning door in front of you? Are you ready to offer your intention and earn it?

We make our most important decisions intuitively, and then the brain tries to execute with logic and reason. It does not matter what state your life or relationships are in right now, set an intention to earn an entirely new kind of love in your life. Trust your intuition.

Decide. Open the Door.

Say yes to an authentic life, not a safe one.

Standing still with your hand on the doorknob will never show you what you are fully capable of. Love is about taking risks. Once you decide to open that door, the journey to what we call belovedness can begin. You may look right now at the person lying next to you in bed, and realize they are your one-and-only-super-duper-beloved.

Or, maybe you know deep in your heart that your beloved is somewhere out there waiting for you. Maybe they are making the same momentous decisions that you are to find each other. We know you are terrified, but do it anyway. Decide that you are worth it. You intend to be worth it. Relationship is worth it. Love is worth it. Circumstances do not matter. Time does not matter. Becoming a student of love opens up all sorts of doors. All is possible.

And when two such people encounter each other, the past and the future become unimportant. There is only that moment, and the incredible certainty that everything under the sun has been written by one hand only. It is the hand that evokes love... Something older than humanity, more ancient than the desert. What the boy felt at that moment was that he was in the presence of the only woman in his life, and that, with no need for words, she recognized the same thing. Because when you know the language, it's easy to understand that someone in the world awaits you, whether it's in the middle of the desert or in some great city.

– Paolo Coelho

One of the most fundamental aspects to having a successful, potent and extraordinary love is to have two people share an alignment of mindset. Both are willing to show up, play big, roll up their sleeves, and aim high. If one partner is a seeker and desires growth while the other is stuck and stubborn, troubles will undoubtedly arise. Resigning to an unconscious relationship that just hopes for the best, well, the results are what you'd expect.

Reflection
Close your eyes and imagine a decision you could make to change the way you love or receive love from another? What instantly comes to mind?

Intention is a key to taking that first step and walking through the door, but your mindset has a great deal to do with how the journey will unfold. In her book, *Growth Mindset,* Professor Carol Dweck of Stanford University outlines two very different ways in which humans approach the world: growth or fixed mindset.

A growth mindset is "the understanding that abilities and understanding can be developed" says Dweck. Those with a growth mindset believe that they can become smarter, more intelligent, and more talented through putting in time and effort towards the goals they have set.

On the flipside, a fixed mindset is one that assumes that abilities, understanding, capacity and achievement are immutable. Those with a fixed mindset believe that you either "have it or you don't" when it comes to abilities and talents. And love.

When we were children, our mindset was always open. We were happy to jump into play and always eager to try new things. Children fundamentally have a growth mindset. As we age, we allow our perspective to become more static. We equate uncertainty or mistakes with failure, and avoid circumstances that could make us look weak, incompetent or bad at something.

The idea that we are either good at something or not, or that it is too late to learn something new is based in fear. A fixed mindset hides flaws, avoids challenges, and ignores feedback that could be felt as personal criticism. That is not going to get you very far in life or love. With time, practice and patience, we can learn anything, and being a dedicated discoverer is one of the keys to a healthy and happy life. As Pablo Picasso said, "All children are born artists, the problem is to remain an artist as we grow up."

A growth mindset is creativity, resilience, open-mindedness, and optimism. It is fascinating to note the mindset many people have about relationships. Rather than approaching from a perspective of growth, most people are not only fixed, they are cemented. See if you recognize any of these examples:

- "I can't make this any better, it is what it is."

- "Oh, you guys just met? Yeah, just wait until you move in together."

- "Well, you may be happy now, but all that lovey-dovey stuff will wear off soon enough."

- "He/she will never change."

Developing and maintaining a growth mindset in a relationship is a rebel move. It is bold, daring and free. Don't be afraid to forge new ground.

Reflection
Where do you see a fixed mindset holding you back in love and in creating a more conscious relationship?

Earning love will require you to examine yourself, your partner and the state of your relationship. Everyone has room to move on the spectrum from a fixed to a growth mindset. For the moment, don't worry about where your partner is, just think about your place on that range. See where you have that little voice of judgement, restriction, or resignation, and make a conscious choice to look at it differently from the perspective of growth.

Big life transitions can destabilize us and test our mindset. Fixed mindset means safety. Yet all the magic lies in the growing unknown. Expanding yourself into a growth mindset and opening up to look at your own potential is core to evolving your love and relationships.

When both partners have a growth mindset, they can learn and do anything they apply themselves to. From a growth perspective in love, it is possible to make a new type of commitment that feels effortless, precisely because you are no longer attached to a fixed expectation or outcome. Beloved couples make mistakes, they work hard, they disagree, they try new things, they win, they have setbacks, and they are inspired by each other.

One of our favorite beloved couples is Ellen DeGeneres and Portia de Rossi. Married for over a decade, they have inspired millions to embrace all relationships as simply, "love is love."

Portia understands me completely. In our vows, she recited a quote - 'It is good to be loved. It is profound to be understood' - and to me, that's everything. What 'I love you' really means is 'I understand you,' and she loves me for everything that I am.

— Ellen DeGeneres

Conscious couples flourish precisely because they share a growth mindset about each other, and about the relationship they share. Not only are they attentive to the day-to-day aspects of life as a couple, but they also play, celebrate, create, and refuse to give in to the mundane.

Reflection
Take a moment and reflect on what aspect of love and relationships you want to build or enhance from a growth mindset. Have fun with the possibilities!

A couple living by the "old rules" is a partnership that limps along, without a mission or purpose beyond the effort required to make it from day-to-day or month-to-month. Neither partner particularly likes it. Yet many stay there for decades assuming there is just nothing left to do. Having a growth mindset between beloveds looks very different.

- They always seem to be positive with each other, no matter how long they have been together.

- They may disagree, but they never disparage one another.

- They feel each other's rhythm in almost a prescient manner, and often touch or connect throughout the day.

- They clearly feel at home in each other.

Beloved couples inspire others around them by the sheer audacity of displaying their love for one another for the entire world to see. From this place, the adventure truly begins.

All the possibilities of your human destiny are asleep in your soul. You are here to realize and honor these possibilities.
– John O'Donohue

Now that you have updated your growth mindset, you can more easily walk through the door into a brand-new adventure. You can begin your journey for you and for your relationship. There is greatness inside of you, lured by love. Let's find it, and then share that adventure with your beloved.

A hero's journey always begins by acknowledging the ordinary world and then hearing the call for adventure from somewhere deep inside. The knowing that you are ready for something more. You may be in the midst of a change, yet still have no idea what is next for you.

Perhaps like many, you feel a sense of merely existing or coasting along, trying to keep stress and overwhelm at bay. You are getting by, systematically knocking down the to-do list day after day. Yet somehow you know there is more, and life is short. Some bigger force is whispering in your ear. It is a call you would be foolish to deny.

The big question is whether you are going to be able to say a hearty "yes" to your adventure.
– Joseph Campbell

One of the reasons you may be exploring this book is that you feel there is something next in your life, a voice telling you that there is still something left to do, to experience, to become. More.

It is easy to disregard this whisper and avoid attending to your inner journey. Why not push off this call to adventure for another time when life is calmer? It is simpler to ignore life's grand nudges, or put them off. Who has time? It is so much easier to wait until next year, or when the kids graduate, or when there is more money in the bank.

You know what you have to do in order to step up to your full potential, both as an individual, and also in your ability to become a beloved to another. Perhaps your intuition is telling you that the time is now. You just need to be given explicit permission.

Seriously. Go for it. You have our permission. Don't live with regrets. Your call to adventure awaits.

Joseph Campbell famously coined the phrase, "Hero's Journey" in 1949, and released his magnificent PBS series on the subject with Bill Moyers in 1987. His work refers to a wide-ranging category of tales in which a hero ventures out, faces mysteries, obstacles and conflict, and ultimately triumphs over adversity and returns home with newfound knowledge and wisdom. It begins with a "Call to Adventure," and departure from the familiar world, followed by an initiation into the unknown, and a triumphant and blissful return. This adventure can be your love story as well.

Campbell described the hero's journey's ultimate outcome of adventuring within yourself and gaining a new level of wisdom. The purpose is to let go of the old, face your fears, and evolve by crossing the threshold.

We must let go of the life we have planned, and accept
the one that is waiting for us.
– Joseph Campbell

This is precisely the journey of Becoming Beloveds. Your call to adventure, your hero's journey, your bliss awaits. Throughout your life you have been preparing to reach this very moment. You are ready.

Once you say yes, doors will open to celebrate your choice. Signs will appear to reinforce your decision. Magic will be afoot. You will earn great rewards.

As you open the door and begin your journey, the path ahead may look arduous. There will be challenges. Each one will help you to raise your consciousness and awareness about yourself and about relationships. Still, you have trepidation.

But wait!

All the best journeys begin with a talisman or charm to slip in your pocket, or a secret password that gives you the confidence to step through the door. Our gift is a secret phrase to use as an anchor for when you are feeling fixed in your mindset, uncertain, or wondering if you've lost your way.

Write it down. Slip it into your pocket like a secret gem or a golden coin. Ready?

Love is Easy + Love is All

It is meant to be easy, but understanding this talisman takes effort.

Go ahead and whisper it to yourself, say it out loud. Say it to your partner and agree to hold it sacred.

After all: Love *IS* easy.

It can be easy like breathing. It can be effortless. Love flows in, around and through you. It is expansive. It creates possibility. It flows.

And, in the most generative sense: Love *IS* all.

It is all that matters. It is the center and the core, the beginning and the end. It is what we want. Everything else is just background noise. This is the pure and peaceful place we all want to call home.

You may not think you need such reminders, or a trite talisman for such an illustrious journey. But make no mistake, it is far from trite. This hero's journey to become Beloveds is the real deal. It will become the most important journey of your life. It is worth fighting every dragon, swallowing every form of fear or self-doubt, and reaching for the brass ring.

Sure. It won't be a breeze. There will be cynics and skeptics out there who will try to tell you that "Love is hard", or that "Love is gone," or that "Relationships are hard work", or even that "Love stinks."

All you have to do when facing these adversaries is remember your talisman.

Love is Easy + Love is All

Let them laugh. Let them sneer. Secretly, they wish they knew where you were going. You are about to show them what love really looks like. When you get to the summit and look at how far you've traveled and what you've accomplished you will never be the same. You have a talisman to give you strength on the adventure ahead.

If you do follow your bliss you put yourself on a kind of track that has been there all the while, waiting for you, and the life that you ought to be living is the one you are living. Follow your bliss and don't be afraid, doors will open where you didn't know they were going to be.
— Joseph Campbell

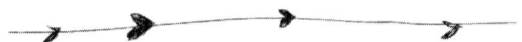

We will offer the wisdom of poets and various wise voices to guide you along the way. Abraham Maslow is one particular sage, a truly enlightened individual, who has clarified the path for us and offered a model we incorporated to evolve in relationships. Maslow, who died in 1970, had devoted his life as a psychologist and philosopher to theories on self-actualization, personal growth, and self-transformation.

He developed a "Hierarchy of Needs" which textbooks usually portray in the shape of a pyramid with our most basic needs at the bottom, and the ideal goal of self-actualization at the top. In later years, Maslow added another level beyond the top of the traditional pyramid called Transcendence.

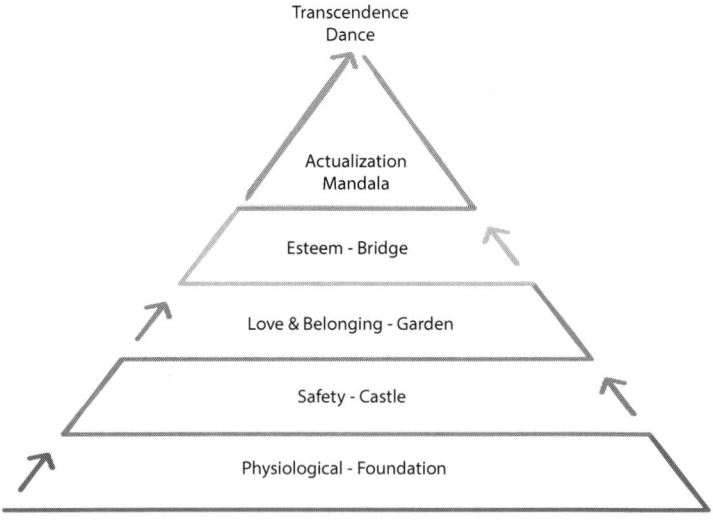

The hierarchy of needs provides an understanding of how humans intrinsically behave when it comes to what we need and what we desire. It has been applied to individuals, groups, businesses and in a minor way to how romantic relationships function. We have found this model provides a great guide to understanding the journey towards Becoming Beloveds.

Maslow's Hierarchy of Needs has been instrumental in helping us elevate our life and create a more conscious love. He can be your relationship guru too. We have applied each level of his hierarchy and philosophy toward couples' development in the following chapters, paired with the stanzas from our poem at the beginning of this book. These levels will be playing a role in your life and in your relationship.

For example, if the bottom level of achieving food, water, warmth and rest is not attended to, nothing much more can happen. If you have experienced a major blood sugar crash or a sleepless night, you know what we mean; processing emotions and ideas becomes very difficult when basic needs are unmet. Developing an awareness of how this level of basic needs plays out in your life offers insight into how you are reacting to your partner and the world around you.

What is necessary to change a person is to change his awareness of himself.
– Abraham Maslow

For us, this psychological pyramid has morphed into a pathway, an adventure and a metaphorical hero's journey. Think of it as a way to frame your explorations and guide your progress toward a more conscious expression of love.

If you take the time to reflect on each of these levels in the chapters ahead, you will be comforted and inspired to realize that we are all struggling at times, we are all growing, and we are all well-intentioned. It may help you to see where you have flourished and where you have neglected certain critical needs in your own evolution.

Reflections that lead to deep and authentic insights are part of why we are here. Life and love are not meant to be cushy or easy. They are meant to be provocative, challenging and evolving. As a couple, no matter how happy, conscious or comfortable you are, this is a toolkit to give your relationship a thorough check-up.

Give yourself and your relationship the gift of self-reflection.

This journey ahead is something each partner must be willing to undertake individually, as well as within your relationship. Ultimately, if we are unable to rise through our own hierarchy of needs, we cannot give ourselves fully to another. No one can drag you up this pyramid. You may want your partner to self-actualize, but if they are unwilling to address their basic foundation the gap between you may become a chasm of constant friction.

However, every couple can begin by reviewing their overall approach to a relationship and begin with the foundation. Both of you had to walk through the doorway to get here. Now you can roll up your sleeves and give your relationship the attention it deserves.

CHAPTER 2

CREATE LOVE ~THE FOUNDATION

*If you have built castles in the air, your work need not be
lost; that is where they should be. Now put the
foundations under them.*
– Henry David Thoreau

What does it feel like to create something? As
children, we loved to draw pictures, play with
dough or build forts using anything at hand. Creating
was as easy and innocent as breathing. It is natural to
want to create. How can this pure impulse be put to use

in relationships? By designing an entirely new paradigm for love. Start to finish.

Throw out all of your preconceived notions and begin again. Find a new piece of land and start designing your beloved dream house. Grab a sketchpad, some pencils and outline a new relationship landscape by design and not by default or random circumstance. Add brilliant color and detail to the vision of your imagination. But before you lay the foundation or stretch that canvas, you need to think about the tools you plan to use.

What emotional tools or values in relationships have served you in the past, like curiosity or patience? Which have caused stagnation and decline in your relationship, like stubbornness or righteousness? Remember your growth mindset and your talisman as you prepare to throw out the broken crayons and start with a fresh new box.

Keep in mind that your journey is to throw out old labels and evolve as an individual or a couple right now. Don't forget that you are an adventurous hero on a quest.

 ***Reflection***
What qualities would you want to create in a new foundation of love?

As you begin to dig the foundation of your new relationship dream house, ask yourself what aspects or qualities create the bedrock of beloved love?

Though it may not be easy, nothing will change until you take a fresh look at your foundation, at that which lies hidden beneath. Deep in your unconscious you may have formed habits that have brought suffering and pain in love and relationships. Maybe you inherited those habits, maybe you simply got lazy, or maybe you just weren't prepared to take the leap of faith and consciousness that this journey requires. Take heart: the very fact that you are reading this book means you are ready now.

Have you ever watched a house being built? For the longest time, it seems as if nothing is happening. But in fact, everything that matters IS happening. Out of sight, plans, designs, measurements and assessments are being made. Then one day the cement is poured and critical supports and beams are put in place. And then the rest of the house goes up in no time.

A house hastily built on quicksand is obviously not one that will last. A relationship based on a quick fix to soothe an unconscious wound will likewise sink into the muck. In order to build something that endures, you are going to need a strong foundation of who you are and what your relationship means in the highest and purest sense. Each individual must have a strong inner foundation in order to create solid footing as a couple. One cannot exist without the other. Together, use your inner strengths to create a new and robust base of connection that can withstand storms, winds of change, and external pressures. Creating this couple foundation requires a strong and sturdy inner fortitude, and a willingness to rethink the environment around you and the way you interact within it.

The great pyramids of Egypt were thoughtfully designed, stone by stone, and have stood for thousands of years. Ancient castles stand today because their foundation is formidably solid. The base of a beloved relationship is deliberately and artfully designed to withstand external forces. There is a certainty that both of you can overcome the inevitable travails of job losses or changes, internal shocks of family illness or death, and the unavoidable effects of time on our bodies and dreams.

Bases of pyramids are the thickest, strongest (and sometimes the most plain) for a reason. They have to support all the levels and intricacies built above. The foundation of a building is not always obvious. Yet, even if we can't see it, if it is not properly built it will topple. This is also true for your relationship. Getting a handle on the basics may not seem sexy or sublime, but neither is the heavy stone at the base of the pyramid. Reviewing your foundation consistently will help to prepare for any fundamental cracks that could become a problem as you progress.

What is the purpose of a home? It is a place we protect ourselves from the elements, a place to sleep and rest. It is a place to nourish ourselves with various kinds of sustenance. Sometimes it is a place to be social, and often a place for privacy and solitude.

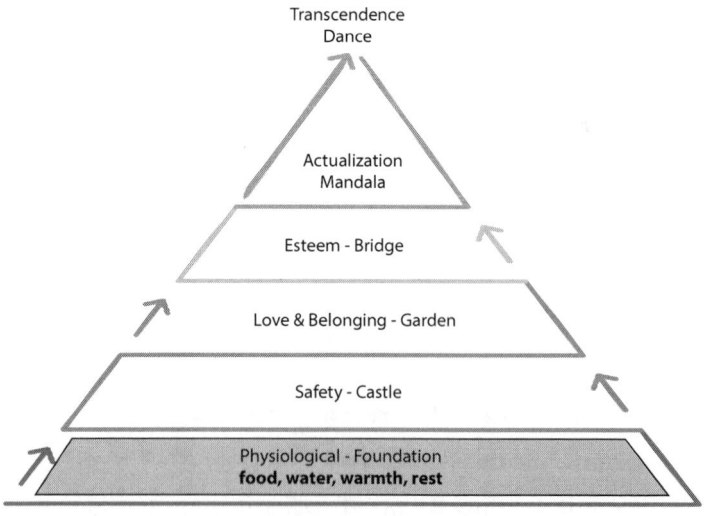

The first level of Maslow's pyramid reflects these basics; the most primal human drives that require daily attention: food, water, sleep, and shelter. This is what we need to stay alive at the most fundamental level. Maslow had strong thoughts about this first level of the relationship hierarchy and the need to master this before progressing onward and upward.

Let's bring out a few more sophisticated tools and break down the foundation level into two key elements: the physiological basics and the primary roles within the relationship.

Physiological Basics:

It does not matter if you are sharing a room or a mansion, how you create and prioritize your physical and emotional space is essential. Physiological basics are the foundation of your relationship and so much more than simple shelter. Keeping your physical space solid and supportive is of primary importance. This is the base you both need to feel secure, and without which it would be difficult to progress to the next levels on your beloved journey.

Relationship Roles:

In any committed relationship, creating a solid foundation begins and sometimes ends by how well you understand the many different roles you and your partner play, the tasks and duties you adopt. Rather than assuming these roles by default, beloveds address them mindfully. Think of these relationship roles as the support beams that rise from the base. In designing your more conscious and evolved relationship, each individual has responsibilities. In which do you feel the most competent or inadequate? Which do you adore or secretly resent? Building a new house with a solid foundation requires a collaborative balance of talents and skills.

Paying attention to these simple elements with a different awareness transforms them into the most wonderful building blocks to create a more conscious perspective individually and in relationship. The process of Becoming Beloveds begins by establishing a mindful foundation that allows each of you to rise above and beyond the mundane and routine. Allow your adventure to challenge you to elevate and celebrate the basics of *shelter, food,* and *sleep* as three critical tools to mix your foundational concrete. The more attention you pay to these basics - simple as they may seem at first - the easier it will be to feel relaxed, centered, and grounded at home.

Tool #1: Shelter - The Container

Remember that simple shelter is crucial to begin any journey towards self-actualization and in our view, critical to your advancement as a couple. Take some time to survey your overall physical environment with fresh eyes. A chaotic space is stressful. Yet partners may have different tolerances for how a disorganized environment makes them feel. If one partner is more sensitive to dust, dirt or disorder, this doesn't go away, even if the other partner really doesn't mind.

Walk into your living space with fresh eyes. How does it feel when you walk in? What emotions does it evoke in you? Do you feel stressed and instantly overwhelmed with tasks to attend to or does it invite sighs of relief? This matters more than we realize. Taking the time to design your home to be your container, your incubator, your retreat allows you to take on the outside world from a place of balance.

Clear the clutter, take the time to put a few special things out that inspire you and transform your home into a sacred space. Note that each of you must find your own definition of what that means and find a way to deeply honor each other's needs.

If you know that your partner gets flustered by a messy house, then THAT is the reason you want to be sure that it is orderly and fresh. We're not talking about daily spotlessness, just the few minutes it takes to tidy up so your partner will come home, look around, exhale with joy, and leap into your arms. It's worth it.

Because it is not about the house. It is about your foundation as a couple. We are not talking about one person constantly being the housekeeper. What is critical is your active participation and attention to your shared environment.

Reflection
When you think of your current living space, what adjectives come to mind? What can you do to transform your space into a sweet container you adore?

Tool #2: Food & Nourishment - The Comfort

Our bodies require food to survive, but it is so much more than simple fuel. It is fragrant memories linked to favorite dishes, holiday meals, midnight snacks or grandma's secret meatball recipe. Home equals hearth truly means all that and more. It is those special smells or simmering sounds we experience when walking in the door that instantly equate to relaxation, calm and connecting with those we love. These days home and hearth are becoming more fragmented. Our culture offers us detours, distractions and so many ways to be unconscious and disconnected about how we satisfy this basic need.

Food has become, in many ways, a convenience product, but the difference between wolfing down a "convenient" bag of fast food from the drive-through, or savoring a meal prepared with care and attention by someone you love is huge. Fast food feels like a lead ball in your stomach. A two-minute speedy microwave dinner is not much better. The option of a lovely home-cooked meal is a healthy gift. It is (usually) delicious and comes with the delightful bonus of good conversation while the meal is prepared, shared and savored.

Gutball or gift, which would you choose? Whether or not you cook, investing time and interest in every aspect of sharing food as a couple is foundational. Yes, we know, everyone is busy; but this is crucial stuff, and can make a huge difference in lifting body, mind, and spirit. Take some time, slow down, cook, converse and enjoy the benefits of an excellent meal together.

How do you and your partner attend to each other and your environment when it comes to food and cooking? Of course, there are always the staples needed to run a household, but we are talking beyond basics.

What can you do every day to elevate the beauty of nourishing one another? Even if one of you is a better cook than the other, is there a collaborative attitude about food and the role of the kitchen as your hearth? Are you each taking responsibility for meal planning, shopping, cooking, and cleaning up? Do you both attend to the environment around meals or do you just assume it will happen somehow?

Assumptions get partnerships into trouble. Many couples struggle at this basic level because they do not articulate their thoughts and needs around food. Simple tasks such as managing the pantry, fridge, and table can become a battleground if couples do not make an effort to understand what is important to each other.

Exploring a more conscious relationship to food and the connective power of the kitchen will have an impact on how you see the world and will transform the depth of your beloved foundation.

Creating rituals around food can be very empowering.

Consider the following questions:

What is your favorite ritual of the day when it comes to food or drinks?

For some it is the first cup of coffee in the morning. If that is the case, how can you savor and ritualize it even more? Splurge on the highest quality coffee and a special mug that delights you every day. If you love tea, invest in fragrant loose-leaf teas, gourmet honey, and a brewing pot. Maybe your favorite food is your small bowl of ice cream before bed. Voila! Don't settle for the cheapo gallon on sale. Indulge. Get that yummy pint of gelato. Buy an awesome ice cream scooper and find a gorgeous but small sized special bowl to give you just enough to satisfy.

Now, think about your partner. What do they love? How can you create opportunities to enjoy food together?

Paying attention to your partner's food and drink ritual favorites and creating new ones together is a powerful way to build your relationship. Figuring out the things your partner loves, and stocking the cabinets with those favorites is a simple but meaningful gesture.

Celebrate meals instead of rushing through them. In the evening, or at breakfast, play some music, dance around the kitchen and put together a lovely meal to share. Take part in the preparation while sharing the stories of the day or night before. This doesn't have to be every day, but it could be if you wanted; why not? Infusing your meals with loving intention offers opportunities to connect, bond, and relax into the comfort of home. Make a small investment in cloth napkins and candles. Put some flowers in a vase. When we pay a little bit more attention, the soul thrives and we feel truly nourished instead of conveniently fed. Hearth is where the heart is.

There is nothing that can make you feel more loved by your partner than everyday nourishment. We are not suggesting catering to every whim. Rather, make the small and pleasurable effort to understand your beloved's preferences. Create an environment where you can share in the loving rituals of food.

Reflection
Take a moment to reflect on your favorite memories related to food or a special meal. What are they?

Tool #3: Sleep - The Connection

Now let's talk about another important part of Maslow's first physiological level of self-care: sleep. Everyone needs a certain amount of sleep to survive, but unsatisfying slumber over time will erode your health physically and mentally. For couples, each partner's quality of rest is very important.

There is nothing yummier than getting cozy with the one you love, curling up together, sighing as the sheets envelop you, and whispering goodnights draped in each other's arms.

Well, for some. Others will snuggle for a minute but then opt for some space to spread out and snooze without arms wrapped around them. However your preferences work, ensuring both of you have restful sleep is a big priority.

Is one of you sleepless while the other snores? Is one of you staying up late watching TV while the other is waiting for quiet and darkness? Couples can have astonishingly different sleep needs. One person needs hot, another cold. One person needs complete darkness while the other prefers some sort of night-light. Noticing and prioritizing what your partner needs for sleep is vital. Consciously discussing these preferences makes a huge difference. It's not about complaining or whining; it's about being thoughtful and mindful of how important this part of your life together is. Attending to your partner when it comes to getting good sleep can become a primary connection tool.

Sleep can be so much sweeter when it becomes a ritual for conscious couples to attend to with loving care. Just like food, it can be something we pay minimal attention to, or something we can infuse with intention, positivity, and grace on our upward journey of love.

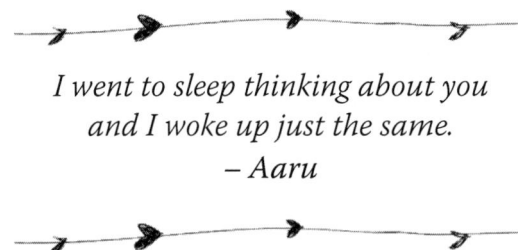

I went to sleep thinking about you
and I woke up just the same.
– Aaru

Just like the kitchen and dining room, the bedroom is an environment that can either be conscious or unconscious and affects us more than we realize. Is your bedroom a sanctuary, or is it a mess? Do you have random stuff and clothes everywhere, with dust on the nightstand and rumpled sheets? Is the big bright TV in your bedroom serving as the evening ritual every night before bed? Does your bedroom feel welcoming and cozy, or chaotic with devices blinking or buzzing?

Think of your bedroom as a sanctuary. It should not be a place that doubles as an office, laundry center, homework station, media hub, and art studio. The bedroom is a sacred nest for beloved couples, and feels so much better when it is a protected space for proper rest, rejuvenation, and intimacy. Being mindful of both the environment of the space and the habits you practice before sleep are surprisingly fundamental to upward growth as a couple.

How do you approach this foundational ritual with your partner? Do you go to bed at night in bulky sweats and spend your final moments watching a war movie, or playing Candy Crush, only to turn out the light, roll over and drift off to sleep with the Grand Canyon between you? How you prepare your bedroom, and how you prioritize being with your partner before sleep is a conscious choice. Make it more loving.

Imagine what happens when you create your bedroom and evening rituals as conscious couples, as beloveds. You make sure this room is a lovely sanctuary that elicits a sigh of relief when you walk in. It is private, sensuous and relaxing. Preparing for bed can include a few extra minutes to light candles, maybe hop in the shower together for a warm rinse and soapy lather as you wash off the day.

Ditch the pajamas and go to bed naked, snuggle skin to skin. Studies by the National Sleep Foundation show sleeping naked helps you fall asleep faster and snooze more soundly. Other studies show those who sleep naked are happier in their relationship. Skin-to-skin contact reduces stress and anxiety. Oh, and couples who sleep naked have more sex, just saying.

Whether you end the night with sex does not matter, yet a healthy sex life overall will lead to better sleep and vice-versa. If sex or sleep is suffering, chances are that one can be bettered by improving the other. It is the intention you give to one another as a priority that makes the difference. It builds a web of comfort and sets the stage for restful sleep.

According to Psychology Today:

Research has shown that sex before bed can help improve sleep quality thanks to the endorphins released by sex, which serve to ease anxiety and relax you. And all of that great sleep can subsequently improve your relationship with your significant other. Sex also releases oxytocin, a hormone known as the "love hormone," which has numerous benefits to your body and mind, including cueing relaxation. "This hormone among many other feel-good hormones has been said to act as a sedative to reduce the time it takes to fall asleep," says Michele Lastella, Ph.D., a sleep scientist at Central Queensland University in Adelaide, Australia.

Reflection
When thinking about these three basic tools of shelter, food, and sleep what roles are they playing in your life? Are you attending to them with care or disregard?

The physiological needs outlined above represent the inner foundation required to build a dream life. Next come the support beams, which for us are the roles we play to keep that foundation solid. Money has to be made, trash has to be emptied, dishes have to be washed, clothes folded, children bathed, bills paid, and lawns mowed. Within an intimate relationship, there are many roles we play to keep our foundation settled that are largely unconscious. We all have many roles we play every single day in life.

Many traditional relationships settle and remain stuck in roles where each partner assumes a series of responsibilities, whether they like them, prefer them, resent them, or not. Couples juggle the various jobs of partner, parent, lover, breadwinner, cook, shopper, bill payer, housekeeper, gardener, trash-taker-outer, bed maker, boo-boo kisser etc. These roles can be a source of tremendous comfort and support that allow each partner to flourish. They can also become a constricting source of miscommunication and disagreements.

Arguments around inherited roles are rampant in relationships. The more that expectations are unbalanced, the greater the threat to the stability of your structure. Sometimes the basic tasks of life are assigned into roles consciously, but usually not. The assignment of these roles is left to tradition or routine. It is time to appraise and then raise our supportive roles in relationships to higher standards on our beloved journey. As a couple, before you can even think about rising in love, the basics of your responsibilities have to be addressed. If you are not in a relationship right now, think about the roles you want to play in your life, with or without a partner.

Take time right now to decide to heighten your standards and consciously create new pillars as thoughtful roles for your foundation. Decide to consciously look at any fixed mindsets you may have about your roles and create new ones. This can be done in so many ways that are actually fun! Get creative, be open and remember it is all about growth.

Artfully and intentionally explore how to transform everyday roles and responsibilities. If you feel insecure about cooking and always leave that to your partner, learn to whip something up! Surprise your partner by watching a cooking show and making that dish. If you think you have a black thumb, shift your mindset and plant a baby box garden next spring.

Couples can engage by sharing their inherent strengths and gently encouraging each other to stretch and grow. Try new roles together each year. Become beekeepers, learn how to make homemade jam, maybe build a kite. There are endless possibilities to transform roles to encourage connection and growth.

Reflection
Without judgment, write down your roles in current or past relationships. If you review them now more consciously, what insights emerge? How could you look at them differently?

One of our favorite ways to turn an ordinary moment or a daily routine into something special is to "cast a spell." Even at this first not-so-magical level of our basic needs, we can cast spells by creating something special out of the ordinary. You can decide that food, sleep and your physical environment are not just basic, boring needs, they are in fact wonderful new tools to create magic.

They are toys in a brand-new playground, an emporium of loving enchantment. This is your opportunity to coax magic out of the most ordinary of moments. Heck, scented candles and sexy music will transform that basic meal or bath into a special moment not soon forgotten.

It is as easy as taking an inventory of your senses with the intention of doing something out of the ordinary and transformative with each.

- **Sight and Light:** Get a few dimmers and turn down bright lights. Make entering your space a unique experience. See what the room looks and feels like in candlelight. Open the curtains to catch the sunlight, or the glow of the moon.

- **Sound:** When you walk into a room, it can be quiet, or you can make a conscious decision to change the tone. Everything from ocean sounds, classical music or hard rock. You pick. But make a choice and transform your environment into an immersive auditory experience.

- **Scent:** We forget about our nose, especially at home. That is until a certain magical scent wafts in. Whether it is freshly-baked cookies, the perfume or cologne of your Beloved, or just a whiff from an aromatherapy diffuser. Pay attention. Infuse your home with scented flowers, or fragrances that you both enjoy.

- **Taste:** Challenge your taste buds now and then. Investigate new flavors and invest in high quality foods. Go to a market and try some samples, or practice a new recipe after watching a cooking show together. Decide to cast a spell at home for everyday meals, not just for special occasions. Fashion a lovely plate and make every meal a special occasion if you can!

- **Touch:** Think about children who love their soft blankies and plush toys. It never really changes, does it? Bring out the soft blankets. Wear luxurious and sensual fabrics. Use coasters to give your table a more finished look. Bring out the crystal glasses and use them on regular occasions. Give your fingers the gift of caressing a different surface than you are used to.

All of these are simple ways to cast a spell in your environment. Once you have decided that you want this magic for yourself and your beloved, you'll never go back to ordinary, it's just not as much fun. Use these simple creative spells of thoughtfulness to create a new kind of love and to bolster your foundation. The gestures may seem small, but so are the grains of sand used to make the cement that is the foundation of your home.

CHAPTER 3

BUILD LOVE ~ THE CASTLE

Where love is deep, much can be accomplished.
- Matsuo Basho

We construct our lives, build our dreams and plan our careers with methodical care. We build our portfolios and families and futures, and yet, how often do we think about actively building a solid and connected relationship? Let's use this question and the impulse to build as inspiration for the next steps on our journey.

Now that your foundation is laid and the support beams are in place, it is time to build something magical. Be sure you have examined and explored the critical components of your foundation before going forward. A house becomes a home when it is buttressed with love and intention.

Have you ever visited a special home and felt relaxed, calmed and happy the moment you walked in? Something about the soothing design, the artful placement of treasures, and the atmosphere in general just made you feel welcome and inspired? Have you ever toured a fabulous mansion, penthouse suite or vacation home that literally took your breath away? That is what we are going for next. Are you ready? Why settle for a tent when you can build a castle of beloved love.

Reflection
Think back to all of the most magical places you have visited in your life. What made them so memorable? If you could have any dream home, what would it be? A ranch, a log cabin, a beach house or a villa?

A castle is a wondrous symbol of shelter, beauty and inspiration, and is a perfect metaphor on the upward journey to Becoming Beloveds. It is a magical place to live and to feel protected and safe. The time and care taken to craft your home on the inside and out matters. Think back to the three little pigs. You know the story. The first little pig made his house out of straw lickety-split. The second little pig decided to go sturdier and built his house out of sticks. While it did take him a bit longer, the overall lack of foundation and attention made it highly vulnerable. The third little pig designed his house with care. He chose his materials thoughtfully and took the time to design and construct his home brick-by-brick. While his brothers were goofing around and mocking him, he paid no attention. His castle was his only focus.

When the big bad wolf showed up and approached the houses of straw and sticks, it took barely a huff and a puff to scatter both to the wind. Pig number three was prepared and unafraid. He welcomed his two homeless brothers, calmly lit a fire and put on a cauldron of soup. Moments later, the wolf blew at the house of bricks with all the bluster he could muster. And nothing happened. This castle was built to last.

Most of us know how the story ends. Wolf soup for weeks in the safety and security of the family home. Those three little pigs offer a parable for building a strong, long-lasting castle for us and for our beloveds.

Beloveds don't just build a home, they craft a castle fit for proverbial kings and queens. A place of joy, pageantry, security, abundance, art and celebration. No matter the size, value or location of your home, it is how you create and enjoy your environment that makes all the difference. This is one of the most delicious benefits of building a life together.

A castle is not dependent on an exact location. It can be rebuilt and refurbished anytime as long as the work of the foundation is solid. Maybe you want to add a new addition or wing. Maybe a roof is being replaced. At this level of relationship, the projects are shared, brick-by-brick. Individual and shared strengths are highlighted, weaknesses intuitively compensated.

From this protected vantage point, beloveds can explore the nuances of safety. This chapter explores security from multiple viewpoints, and how to be more aware of the impact it has on our general state of mind and the state of our relationship.

Abraham Maslow placed safety on the second tier of his hierarchy of needs. After our basic requirements of food, sleep and physical foundations are met, we must be both physically and emotionally safe in order to thrive and evolve. If we are not feeling safe, nothing higher can be achieved or actualized.

Becoming Beloveds

Transcendence
Dance

Actualization
Mandala

Esteem - Bridge

Love & Belonging - Garden

Safety - Castle
security, safety

Physiological - Foundation

It is not just physical safety from harm that matters. We grow when we are feeling safe physically, emotionally, financially, and psychologically. Let's take some time to understand what Maslow meant when he wrote about the choices we make around safety. There are three main dynamics within the concept:

- Avoiding Mortal Danger

- Steering Clear of Anticipated Danger

- Creating Perceived Safety

Mortal Danger

You know that feeling. The hair on the back of your neck stands up. Your stomach tells you that something is just not right. That's your brain, your gut, your body picking up on your environment and assessing your outer safety or potential for danger. Danger is a situation in which some vital part of you, whether physical, emotional, financial, or spiritual, is put at risk.

Staying away from danger is how we humans have survived and evolved our species. Historically, we have faced all sorts of dangers from other animals, other not-so-nice people, illnesses, and Mother Nature herself. Maslow identifies safety as a key hierarchical need for individuals.

The same is true for couples. Protecting your partner from harm and threats is vital to the basic stability of a relationship. If you don't protect your partner from harm then unnecessary fight or flight responses will erode the relationship.

Anticipated Danger

Most people recognize mortal danger, like drunk driving or dark alleys at 2am. Anticipated danger is more like risk management. It is when you know a hurricane is coming but no one, including your partner, is preparing the house for the oncoming storm. Anticipated danger is when you park your car too far from the concert and have to walk through a dangerous area. The threat itself has not materialized, but the level of fear, matched with a level of unpreparedness, will undercut the most intimate of bonds.

Beloveds not only keep each other out of immediate harm's way, but they ensure that they are safe in the future. A beloved couple anticipates possible threats and prepares for them, so if dangers materialize they are easily handled instead of being caught off guard.

Perceived Safety

Safety is not just physical. Developing a healthy sense of security for individuals and for couples includes both protection from physical danger and an attention to emotional and spiritual safety. This domain requires a subtler awareness. Not just *being* safe but *feeling* safe.

As you are climbing the pyramid, it is vital to develop a nuanced ability to nurture your lover's sense of safety. This is an area of relationship where couples are often unaware, and it can cause all sorts of unintentional pain. When perceived safety is threatened or neglected, even slightly, we often shut down or shut out, we tear each other down and then tear out the door.

Perceived safety is all about how vulnerable you allow yourself to be and feel around your partner.

People don't feel safe when their partner puts them down, or erupts into anger, rage or silence. This puts us on edge, increases our stress hormones and impacts our physical, mental and emotional state. The physiological responses to any kind of fear are similar to those of being in physical danger. You want to flee, you can't relax, and you certainly cannot put yourself in a vulnerable position to be intimate. Perceived danger is as fatal to intimacy as mortal danger.

The complicated thing is that we can feel afraid for a huge variety of reasons. Be comforted by this, because it is manageable when we know what it is. We can feel afraid for all sorts of reasons that have *nothing* to do with being in actual danger. For whatever reason, we may feel afraid when home alone, or when we don't know where our spouse is for a few hours, or when or the car only has a quarter tank of gas; everyone has their unique triggers and fears.

Reflection
Have you experienced a moment when a partner did something sweet and unplanned that made you feel wonderfully safe? What was it? What happens when you feel unsafe even if you are not in physical danger?

Perceived dangers and our emotional responses to them can be very different, even within a couple's domain. Rather than offering a critique, instead, ask your partner to try to explain their fears and insecurities, giving each other the liberating experience of being understood and protected, no matter what. Offer the safety of loving arms in which to be held, without a single word of judgment or outcome needed. In her book *Daring Greatly*, Dr. Brené Brown defines vulnerability as, "uncertainty, risk and emotional exposure." When we are afraid of being judged or not supported, that vulnerability can simply shut us, and our relationship, down.

Keep your momentum going by being the person your partner turns to for reassurance, comfort and calm. Making someone feel safe is not so much fixing a problem as it is offering unconditional love and acceptance. Make them feel safe. Be there for the little things, and do it all the time.

There are little acts of neglect that may seem innocent or simply careless at the time. Yet, when your partner reacts, either by being anxious, or erupting into accusations and defensiveness, the issue at hand is not the small careless act; but rather that a core foundation of safety was threatened.

Building proactive safety is done quietly, sweetly and calmly. It's preparing for storms before they arrive and without a need for acknowledgment. It's a gentle nudge, sometimes physical, sometimes emotional, to guide a partner out of harm's way. Beloveds scan the horizon and guide each other towards the best path, always adjusting and tending to each other's needs and sheltering each other from the storms of life. It's pretty powerful to incorporate these as conscious habits.

Life is an ongoing process of choosing between safety (out of fear or the need for defense) and risk (for the sake of progress and growth). Make the growth choice a dozen times a day.
— Abraham Maslow

Now that the castle is strong and safe, and internal dangers feel understood, it's okay to explore outside a little! Let down the drawbridge and go on an adventure of how beloveds interact. It's time to venture deeper into the forest. Sometimes it could be an ominous and dangerous forest, or it could be enchanted and lovely-depending on how you look at it. Within this forest you will now meet what we call *paper cuts and honey drops.*

Paper-cuts. The dark mist in the forest. Paper cuts are those painful little injuries that come from an innocent-seeming book or envelope and can hurt for days. Relationship paper-cuts don't come from paper, but from our words. They sound innocent enough, but the pain they inflict is deep and lasting. It is an ominous part of the forest of love indeed.

Here's a simple example. You know those little stories when people joke about their partner and how they always forget their keys or their glasses. How they leave their towels on the floor or wear unfashionable clothes and mismatched socks.

It's those stories. Dismissive, passive-aggressive stories partners tell about each other that are cold and dark. People somehow feel compelled to share their partner's little foibles as fodder for ridicule. It's become an acceptable social pastime, practically a sport.

Paper cuts seem innocuous, but boy do they linger and hurt. They show your partner in a bad light. They demonstrate to the world that you are angry and a little bit mean. That somehow it is acceptable to make fun of your partner, in public no less. They are little slashes that leave big wounds. They make your partner feel unsafe around you when you should be the one person they always feel safe around.

Praise in public, critique in private is a time-honored leadership creed and it should be part of how you keep your intimate partner feeling safe. You know why? Because when you critique your partner in public you shame them. It really doesn't feel good for anybody. If you feel the need to voice something that annoys you about your partner, so irksome that you just can't let it go, do it privately, do it lovingly.

There is shame on both sides of a public paper cut. You know you have delivered one when your partner's eyes change and become sad, they retreat, or become defensive. They'll start to justify how their toothpaste squeezing technique is not that bad and how you are making too much of it. Then they will give you a paper cut in return, instinctively finding a way to return the wound you gave to them. The forest gets darker.

Dr. John Gottman is a well-known therapist who famously described four primary threats to any relationship that he called "The Four Horsemen of the Apocalypse". They are comprised of:

- Criticism
- Defensiveness
- Contempt
- Stonewalling

Gottman could pretty much predict divorce based on how many horsemen were allowed to pass into the castle. These are the behaviors that will destroy a relationship. Right there at the top is criticism. Criticizing your partner is an attack on their core character. That is what paper cuts do: they criticize your partner's character, creating shame, defensiveness, and insecurity. When enough of these paper cuts are struck on both sides, the relationship will bleed out. At some point, someone will tire of the knife fight, leave the forest altogether and walk away.

Reflection
Think about a time someone made a sarcastic comment about you. How did you feel? Now think about a time you gave someone else a paper cut. Underneath the laughter, how did it feel deep down to do that to someone else?

Have you ever been out to dinner with another couple and had to endure the uncomfortable-ness when they start bickering with each other and slinging paper cuts, completely unaware of the impact it is having on the evening?

One of the most intense examples of paper cuts we've experienced was at a restaurant that features dining in the dark. The place is pitch black, allowing other senses to be heightened. It was a special evening and we were treating ourselves to something different. Unfortunately, the couple at a nearby table were in the middle of a vicious squabble. Without any visual cues to notice other people's reactions, or the stricken or angry face of their target, their voices continued to rise, and their jabs escalated into a paper cut massacre. Talk about being lost in an evil forest. It was not our idea of a romantic night out.

Those jabs couples throw at each other serve no positive purpose. Don't feel bad if you've done it in the past; most of us have. Sometimes we don't even recognize that we are doing it until the words have left our mouths. It is time to be more conscious of not only our words, but our actions.

Beloveds don't cut each other down. They never intend a paper cut, and if they wound unintentionally, they make amends. Beloveds recognize and are conscious not to slice up their relationship. So, what is the opposite of a paper cut? We call it a honey drop. An enchanted forest filled with magic orbs of golden light.

Instead of our earlier example, imagine going out to dinner with another couple who enjoy one of those rare relationships you deeply admire. The atmosphere is relaxed and easy. Both of them are smiling, connected and close. As the conversation evolves, each of them says something positive about the other. Perhaps as simple as, "she started a new project last month and boy is she crushing it." Later in the evening, she notices that her partner does not seem to be enjoying his meal, so she shares hers without missing a beat of the conversation. They just glow and everyone feels it.

Those are honey drops. Soothing little moments or gestures that reflect you are paying attention to your partner and prioritizing their security and comfort. Why do we call them honey drops you ask? We are huge fans of honey. Honey itself is such a universally sweet elixir and it even has healing properties. Honey drops are the perfect salve for paper cuts. Golden light.

A honey drop is just a little thing. A thoughtful thing. A being-present thing. It is that moment of saying your partner looks great instead of just thinking it. It is that moment of rubbing your partner's back because you want to, and without being asked. It is filling moments with sweetness just because.

And it all ties back into safety. When we cut our partners down, we make them feel unsafe. If we are encouraging and complimentary, we are weaving a lovely web of both security and deep connection. We can skip in the dappled forest light.

Rather than holding onto resentment or sending zingers, do the opposite; send micro-moments of love. That is really what honey drops are. That is really what love is. The fact is, when you think about your partner and ask yourself what you love about them, often the first thing that comes to mind is a brief gesture or behavior of theirs towards you, a little love moment. They link together like a golden daisy chain of thoughtful memories.

Dr. Barbara Fredrickson is a premier researcher in positive psychology and has dedicated intensive study to how we know, understand and experience love. She coined the phrase, "micro-moments" to describe how the brain receives and processes the emotions and gestures of love.

Paper cuts create separation between you and your partner. You are whittling away at them with your words or gestures. Honey drops in the form of micro moments bring you closer together. This changes the wiring of your brain. According to Fredrickson it also literally changes your broader experience of the world.

The inner feeling love brings you is inherently and exquisitely pleasant - it feels extraordinarily good...Yet far beyond feeling good, a micro-moment of love, like other positive emotions, literally changes your mind. It expands your awareness of your surroundings, even your sense of self... While infused with love you see fewer distinctions between you and others. Indeed, your ability to see others... springs open.

– Dr. Barbara Fredrickson

Isn't that exactly what the experience of safety really is? To feel relaxed, open, and expansive. So now it is time for you to decide. Right here, and right now. Decide you will never ever give another person a paper cut.

Get rid of the passive-aggressiveness. Work it out in private. Let your partner shine with you in public. Show the world the lovely sides of your partner. Decide that you want to have your beloved sparkle in how they are reflected in your eyes.

Decide that your beloved will always feel safe by your side. Adore and cherish their most idiosyncratic ways. It is what makes them a perfect human. If you have picked up the nasty habit of slinging paper cuts, just drop it.

Decide to pay attention and just stop. Cold turkey. If you want to build a castle of safety for you and those you love, make sure your surrounding forest is devoid of sharp objects, and filled with magical honey drops.

Strategize on how to sprinkle more honey drops on those you meet throughout your day. Create positive micro-moments everywhere: while in traffic, with the checkout girl taking forever, with your co-workers and your children. Definitely be liberal in drizzling honey drops on your lover. Be audacious in your adoring.

If you decide to drip sweet honey drops in your love forest, not only will you evaporate the dark mist of paper cuts, you will find a partner to share golden daily magnificence. Instead of a painful cut, you will find a blossoming sweetness between you that you never thought possible. You can have any life you want, you just have to decide.

CHAPTER 4

NURTURE LOVE ~ THE GARDEN

The flower doesn't dream of the bee.
It blossoms and the bee comes.
– Mark Nepo

It is a natural instinct for some to nurture; for others, it is more of a learned practice. Yet, most people want to care for something: animals, children, houseplants. Now that your castle is ably built, in this chapter we invite you to become a cosmic gardener. Explore the nature of nurturing as a fundamental component of conscious living and loving. Imagine the Us 2.0 between you and your partner as a garden. What will you plant? Perhaps your garden will feature roses for passion, daisies for joy and lavender for serenity.

As we progress up the hierarchy of love, we begin to explore how beautiful it feels to nurture each other. From the first moments of that dizzying infatuation to the giddiness of making plans for commitment, and into the sweet decades that unfold beyond.

No one teaches couples how to stay "happily ever after." There's no romance school that offers a course for "falling in love over-and-over 101." There's no training to learn the skills or habits you need to attend to a relationship after the honeymoon. Somehow, we are supposed to magically know what it takes to tend to the garden that is our love and relationship.

One reason why we have so much trouble with relationship today may be our neglect of its study. We expect to find intimacy naturally, without education or initiation. When we fail in this area, we assume that we must have some inborn lack. But the fact is, we can do nothing well in life, and that includes intimacy, unless we have the schooled imagination for it.
– Thomas Moore

Like gardens, relationships require active tending and nurturing, even in winter or when the ground is fallow. With your growth mindset firmly in place, you can become a master gardener, seeking to sow the habits it takes to Become Beloveds. You'll have to practice these habits consistently and tend to your beloved garden. But if you do (and if you have read this far then you ARE that kind of person), your garden will flourish.

Filled with color, bursting with life and in constant flux, a garden is a favorite place for the soul to relax and linger. Starting with your rich soil as a pair, plant seeds of love and commitment. A seedling sprouts, then another and another and you have the beginnings of your future together. This must be protected from invaders like weeds or bugs. In time, the garden grows and bursts into a delightful cacophony of blooms, fruits, scents, butterflies and bees.

Love is not something we give or get;
it is something that we nurture and grow, a connection
that can only be cultivated between two people when it
exists within each one of them.
- Brené Brown

A conscious relationship is a garden of perennials that come up over and over again in the form of rituals and traditions, and it is filled with annuals that are the surprising moments each new year brings. Lovers create a garden together filled with rows of special moments, arbors of sweet pet names, beds of shared memories, big adventures, and little gestures.

Beloved love is a gorgeous place for the soul to frolic, play and grow. The fateful spirit that brought the two of you together was profound and mysterious. The magic that causes a seed to sprout and bloom is the same. Let's explore how to nurture your beloved secret garden together.

Tending to a higher-level relationship requires us to think bigger than everyday obligations or passing moods. A beloved love is a living, ever-changing garden and requires lots of fresh air, sunlight, rain and careful tending. In order to fully expand and flourish, the soul garden requires a gamut of encounters and experiences. Go big and plant anything you want.

If you have ever traveled to cooler mountainous areas in spring, you'll see flowers blooming in brilliant contrast to the landscape. They thrive in the dramatic difference of temperatures. A beloved relationship is no different. Your love is not row upon row of pansies, content for a ho-hum, bland and temperate existence. Beloved love requires mystery, surprise, and even an occasional cold snap to evoke the brightest colors and contrasts. Be creative and daring in your planting.

Tending your beloved garden is a delightful way to approach the future with your mate. It invites planning, tending, trimming, and harvesting new projects. It celebrates dreams and goals over and over again.

The more you infuse a lyrical quality into your garden, the richer it becomes. Add a gurgling fountain! Remove the dead bushes that are taking over and plant fruit trees instead. Don't be afraid to start over or prune down to the bottom. This is how new growth happens.

And the secret garden bloomed and bloomed and every morning revealed new miracles.
- Frances Hodgson Burnett

As we rise to the next level in recasting Maslow's hierarchy, we explore our fundamental need for Love & Belonging. Here again we think about giving love (Be Love), and accepting love (Be Loved).

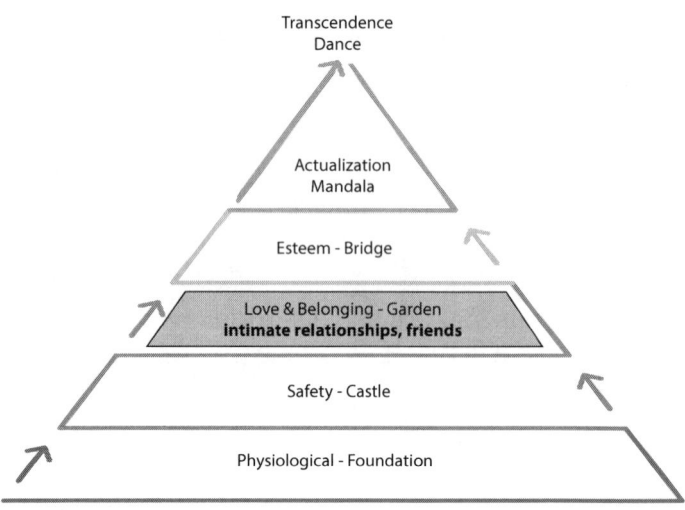

This level of the pyramid is about how you focus on yourself and your partner in creating a dance of intimacy while together and apart. This level is about how you fulfill, support and grow your needs as a couple, and as individuals. After all, plants will wither and die if they are choked out by other invasive plants, or don't receive enough water and sunlight.

We are interactive and tribal creatures. Most of us feel the need to belong to something, to be recognized for who we are, in order to feel safe, secure, and able to further our potential. There are many books out there focused on the importance of building teams and communities, building friendships that last, and finding the fulfillment of social-impact work that you love. For those on the path to Becoming Beloveds, ALL of these areas are vital to embrace.

For most, feeling love is accompanied by a sense of being accepted, wanted, needed, and validated. It is the feeling that you are a part of something greater than yourself. It is no accident that one of the greatest punishments our society inflicts is that of solitary confinement. Being loved, loving, and belonging to a tribe is a core human need. We are social beings, and fundamentally motivated to belong to some sort of group or community with which we connect and identify.

Sadly, the sense of belonging has dwindled within our society and research has shown a rise in loneliness and social isolation, even among those who live with a partner or family. According to one study we read, the impact of identifying as lonely is equivalent to smoking fifteen cigarettes per day, and can reduce a life span by seven years. Experiencing loneliness within the garden of a relationship is dangerous. Left untended, plants wither, wilt, and die.

Reflection
What does it mean to feel like you are loved and truly belong in this world?

How do beloveds manage individual needs for love and belonging, and simultaneously build the bond between them? They pay attention. Paying attention is one of the most caring gifts you can bestow on someone. It means that you have decided that given all the distractions and other things you could focus on, your partner is the most important one. You have decided that what they are interested in is of value to you as well. Not that you have the same affinity or passion for it per se, but that they themselves are worth your time, focus, and attention above all else.

Part of cultivating love and belonging in your garden is recognizing that your partner's needs for social interaction and validation may blend or diverge from your own. Fostering a sense of connection to friends and groups separate from one another is healthy; it creates a flourishing space for independent exploration and growth. If a relationship isolates and excludes itself, that garden will be diminished. Cross-pollination is important.

Your currency for relationship pollination is called "attention," and you can spend it and sow it in so many ways. You can waste it on distractions, you can splurge on fun and leisure, or you can invest it in your relationship. This chapter is about how to deepen the way you pay attention to one another and promote the experience of love and belonging. When you decide that your partner is worth paying attention to, you have told your partner and the world that they are your top priority and you are proud to let everyone know it.

When you decide to spend your attention on them, oh the rewards you will reap. A little uptick in their mood, a soft smile, a knowing glance - it is worth the effort. This is not to suggest that you fawn over your partner's every little behavior. You'll decide the moments and interactions where you want to invest your attention. However, the small moments matter. Sometimes more than the big ones.

You can have any life you want, you just have to decide. Decide to pay attention to your partner.

Having someone pay attention to you, just you, is the foundation of being seen. Especially when that attention is coming from your partner. Imagine your partner noticed something you said or did that was relatively minor. Then at a later time they not only recalled the detail, they paid attention to how important it was to you. It could be as simple as how much you liked that orange scone from the bakery, or how dark you like the roast of your coffee. It could be that next Saturday you know your partner wants to celebrate her best friend's birthday. Without being asked, you arranged for the day to be open and relaxed for them. You set up playdates for the kids, and did the laundry while she was out to lunch. Imagine the response to planting such sweet seeds.

The underlying message is simple: I pay attention to you, because you are worth paying attention to. The decision to pay attention is the decision to see. Your partner has demonstrated that you matter more than anything else when they see you. With all your imperfections, they see you in your full humanity, and in that moment the deep connection is made. You are seen. And loved.

Reflection
Think back to a time someone went out of their way to do something wonderful for you that required paying attention. How did it feel? Do you have that experience now?

Most of us are much better at giving than receiving. Being nurtured can make many feel uncomfortable, guilty, or filled with the need to instantly reciprocate and then some. Oh no. This is not what your lover wants. Just as you want to give to the one you love; conscious partners want to give too.

Receiving is uncomfortable because it requires us to be seen. There is nothing more vulnerable (and more empowering), than truly being seen by another. We have been taught to create all sorts of masks, personae, and traits to help us feel accepted. But that is not the same as being seen. When we are accepted but not seen by our partner, it deadens the relationship.

Gardens are about growth and expansion. This means allowing another to see you, and to bask in this loving sunlight so that you can grow. Every flower, fruit and vegetable is unique. It is about understanding that your partner truly sees you. Allow yourself to be seen. When your partner is paying attention to you, accept it. Enjoy it. Savor it. If you shrug them off or criticize them when they are trying to give you a little love, you are essentially pouring weed killer on your newly thriving roses. Don't do that. Enjoy the ways your partner pays attention to you even if it is different than your own style.

Sometimes we miss these moments because we are wrapped up in ourselves and in the daily dramas that are invading our own little garden. If we forget to focus on what matters, life does tend to creep in and take over like weeds. With all of the distractions we have from social and streaming media, pings and alerts, it is easy to lose focus and let the weeds encroach. If you pay attention to your partner for a minute and then jump back to watching your favorite show, the gesture feels empty. It is not really attention at all.

Reflection
Being present is a practice. How often have you caught yourself in a conversation and not paying attention? How can you be more nurturing to those you love?

You have the power to determine where to direct your attention, and to make thoughtful decisions about prioritizing love, quality time, adventure and play. If you choose to focus on praise, celebration and gratitude, those around you will thrive under such lovely recognition and appreciation. You have the power to pour either poison or vital nutrients into your garden each day. Be present.

Another essential ingredient in growing your beloved garden is time. This is a very precious asset and you must be wise and creative and nourish the seeds together.

Many couples spend hours sharing the same space, but they are not together. They are standing on the same foundation, but are separated by fissures of detachment. One is making dinner, while the other is paying bills. One is tucking in the kids and the other is doing laundry. Even the final precious moments before bed are often spent gazing at some kind of screen before rolling over to sleep. These little disconnects are like weeds that start to take over your garden, grow like mold on your castle walls and create cracks in your foundation. Without proper care, your relationship can be overrun with mundane tasks and separate lives. Romance? Who has time.

Instead of letting time control the relationship, conscious and beloved couples manipulate time to serve their needs. They bend time. Sneaky-smart, right? Try it. Instead of watching a show before bed, sit outside with a blanket cuddling under the stars. Put down the phone and pick up some massage oil. Transform doing the laundry into a weirdly sexy game. You are in control of how you make the most of each and every minute of every day with the one you love.

Prioritizing time to be with your beloved is unusual in our culture. After the early whirlwind of infatuation, many established couples find themselves settling into parallel but separate lives. They go on a vacation where one plays golf and the other goes shopping. Maybe one sits by the pool reading a book while their partner goes scuba diving. The getaway has elements of quality time, but the intention and reward of actual togetherness is missing. Both feel it, and both of you can change it.

Research at the American Psychological Association shows that being a whiz at multitasking can actually reduce efficiency by up to forty percent.

Somehow knowing this and sensing it still doesn't stop us from trying to do too much, too fast, and all at the same time. Many of us are feeling not just time-starved, we are feeling life-starved. Eventually many couples feel relationship-starved as well.

Beloved time is about intentional togetherness - making a decision to be next to and involved with your beloved as a choice against all the other distractions you may have to tempt you. Beloved time implies creating rituals together. Something as mundane as walking the dog or doing the dishes can be turned into beloved time just by ritualizing the process.

Yep, the kids have to get to bed, homework needs to be attended to, the laundry needs to be done. If you ritualize the idea that you and your partner, as a beloved couple, always walk the dog together for seven minutes at night before bed, followed by a quick shower and five minutes of candlelight, you'll be creating beloved time. It's not as difficult as you think.

Truly the joy of nurturing a garden is the joy of procreation. Patiently watching seeds come to bloom and harvest is something akin to pregnancy and birth.

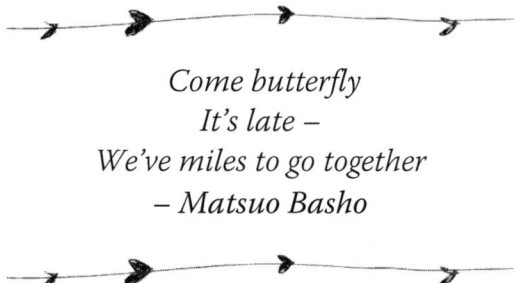

Come butterfly
It's late –
We've miles to go together
– Matsuo Basho

Pregnancy, a long, joyful, creative gestation can be brought to your own life's path and your relationship's soul over and over again. Have proverbial "babies" together again and again. Dream up bucket-list trips, approach that remodeled bathroom as a new pregnancy you get to plan and design together, think of the empty nest as another way to get pregnant with the "What's Next" child of your shared life. Tend to your secret beloved garden. Watch it grow.

Reflection
What projects can you bring to your relationship garden that will keep both of you creative, engaged, planning, sorting and growing together?

Your relationship is not just a long-ago ceremony that is now a set of obligations. It's not about a wooden bowl on your fifth anniversary or a crystal one on your fifteenth. A heightened experience of love is not a steak dinner and roses on Valentine's Day. Real soulful love is tied to magic. It is the fireflies that appear in your garden on a summer evening, or the shooting star that streaks across the night sky. It is the evocation of mystery that sparks renewed passion in the relationship and in one another. It is about feeling rooted and blooming all at once.

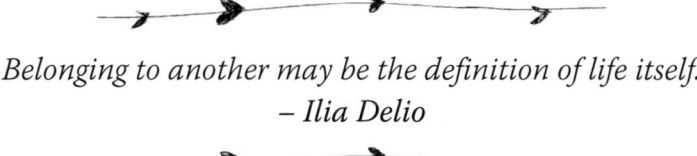

Belonging to another may be the definition of life itself.
– Ilia Delio

What does it mean to belong to someone? Not belonging as in ownership, but rather as a deep spiritual knowledge that you belong together. It is a knowing and a claiming.

"I am my beloved's and my beloved is mine" takes on a truly profound meaning. It is a declaration. We feel held, protected, cradled and yet also free to rise up to who we are meant to become.

Reflection
If you are in a relationship, ask your heart: how do you know that you and your partner belong together?

Knowing that we belong to our partner for all that we are is one of the deepest ways we can experience the true meaning of love. Understanding that our partner loves us in our fear, pain, anger, or thoughtless and regrettable moments, as well as our best moments, offers an incredible sense of peace, and the ability to return this level of unconditional acceptance.

Taking some time to examine how you demonstrate your love to your partner and the ways you help them know viscerally they belong to you cannot be underestimated. Beloved couples often exclaim that their partner "feels like home." This is one of the most profound declarations of love any of us can make.

Part of the beauty of being a committed pair is the ability to love, adore and attend to each other in a way that is exclusive to the two of you. You come to know your partner like no one else does. Only you get to kiss, caress, coo, care for and lift your partner up. Are you taking this job seriously?

Part of belonging together is unconditional acceptance. Each partner has to be vulnerable in showing past wounds that have impacted and shaped them. Faults, mistakes, and misgivings must be shared without fear of judgment. It can be frightening to show your partner how you have been hurt in the past, because it implies you could be hurt again. Growing your garden as a couple means you are safe to process and explore your bruised past and failed projects as tools for reflection and growth.

Breaking up, negative energy, getting divorced, being cheated on, having an affair, being broken-hearted - all of these experiences feel like splitting your soul into a million pieces. The pain is so great, it becomes natural to want to stuff it, forget about it, or just plain ignore it. Yet tilling the soil of our past is part of what creates oxygen and new light. Adding compost to the soil is vital to healthy growth. Shift your mindset. Plant new seeds. Add fertilizer. Grow.

Yet, this is not how most people look at it. Having a splintered romantic past impacts your self-esteem and your ability to understand and accept the potency of belonging again. Sharing your past wounds with your beloved requires trust. When your partner allows you to feel seen and accepted, no matter the emotional scars and bruises, it creates tremendous healing and bonding. Nature understands the power of renewal from what has died. Our hearts require some stress in order to grow.

Telling our stories is a core trait of being human. In wider social circles, we share war stories to secure a sense of tribal acceptance. Mothers do this by swapping details of giving birth or raising children. Professionals in the workforce trade notes on epic office battles. Sharing our difficult stories and our struggles with each other creates empathy and community.

Showing your scars to your tribe is powerful but it takes even more courage to show evidence of your wounds to your beloved. You have to expose the part of you that is most vulnerable: past, present, and future. That takes fortitude and it will be required to have a truly conscious and flourishing love.

When we start to reveal who we are to each other we allow access to the darkest places where we have been burned or cut, are afraid or vulnerable. When we can show each other those old wounds that still sting to this day, it is one of the most vulnerable, and strongest moments of Becoming Beloveds.

This is where the strength of higher love is forged. When you can talk about old romantic connections and where they went wrong, even where they still sting, and realize that your beloved understands and empathizes with you and actively protects that soft spot. You realize, warts, wounds, and all, how much stronger you are together than on your own.

So, show your scars. You don't have to like them or be proud of them, and you don't have to let them define who you are today. But you do have to acknowledge them as part of the unique beauty of who you are, and your partner should know about them in order to understand and care for you. Expose the nooks and crannies of your past and be vulnerable enough to enjoy the soothing strength that grows by this bond.

Reflection
What is a story that you have not wanted to tell your partner? Maybe it is a wound or act you committed you are not proud of. What is at risk by refusing to share your scars?

One of the ways couples devolve in their relationship and destroy the lovely garden they have worked so hard to nurture is by poisoning the garden with separation, the opposite of security and belonging. We withhold our love or push our partners from our inner orbit because we are angry, wounded or resentful. This may seem mild, yet the impact is like a mini-tornado or lightning striking the middle of your garden.

Like "Paper Cuts," those unconscious moments of cutting your partner down, "Lightning Bolts" are those instant decisions we make when we choose not to be close to our partner. Sometimes it is unconscious and other times you may be very deliberately ignoring them, keeping your distance, not answering their calls or texts, or sleeping on the itty-bitty edge of the bed with your back turned. Ouch. Lightning bolts hurt and leave us feeling scorched and separate.

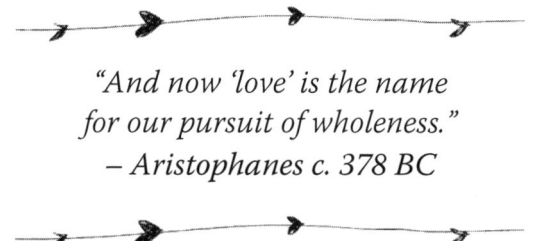

"And now 'love' is the name
for our pursuit of wholeness."
– Aristophanes c. 378 BC

Around 378 B.C. Aristophanes presented a story about the original human beings. These creatures were fleshy orbs fused together, with male and female halves. (Some were made of two females and some made of two males). They had great power and fundamentally knew only union. Instead of walking, they rolled around in grand cartwheels.

Zeus, the king of the gods, felt threatened by these creatures and wanted them to work as slaves, so with a mighty lightning bolt he cut all of the magical humans in two. These new creatures could now walk upright and be put to work. They toiled for the gods and went about life, yet they knew something profound was missing. Their hearts painfully knew longing for their other half, and they used their outstretched arms to search for union, or what we now call love.

We are searching still for our other half and those moments of experiencing wholeness and connection. But we believe there is more to the Aristophanes story. The gods didn't use lightning just to break apart these spherical humans. They also implanted little lightning bolts deep inside the unconscious of these new beings, ensuring that even if a half found its mate, bolts of energy would shoot towards the other and keep them separate.

Moments of finding, recognizing, and declaring love are some of the most profound, powerful, and alluring in all of the human experience. We love those scenes in movies when couples cling to each other in the rain, kissing passionately and confessing their undying love. And then, the lightning bolts. The moments in the rain are replaced with slamming doors, ignoring each other, bickering and sleeping alone on the couch.

We punish our partners in little ways that create big distances. We fixate on the things that separate us instead of those that bring us together. We look at the things our partners aren't doing instead of the things they are doing. It must be their fault, not ours. So, we turn away, fold our arms and reject.

What launches these lightning bolts? Deciding to spend time looking at our phones instead of gazing into each other's eyes. Choosing to come home and go straight to chores instead of pausing for a deep, long, delicious embrace. Going to bed in a sulk instead of talking about what is bothering you. These are little lightning bolts that repel us from each other, and they feel awful because we are meant to be a whole.

When we remove the divisive lightning bolts in a relationship, what we have left are the original sparks. Those joyful moments that light us up with spontaneous play, smiles, giggles, flirtations, and an inner certainty that helps us conquer the world. Sparks should be fanned to fuel the fire of your relationship, supercharge your garden and bolster the entire beloved journey.

Remember your intention is the center of every decision? Remember growth mindset? Bring those tools to right here, and right now, to activate more divine sparks in your relationship. How can you decide to turn toward one another instead of away? Can you set an intention to focus on closing the gap between you and your partner, literally and figuratively?

Divine sparks are so easy to ignite. One playful love tap, one extra-long kiss, an enthusiastic embrace, maybe a quick dance party; they produce instant delight. You will see the divine light in their eyes, and then, enjoy their pleasure.

Let the sparks fly.

"My garden is my most beautiful masterpiece."
– Claude Monet

CHAPTER 5

ELEVATE LOVE ~THE BRIDGE

Love is the bridge between you and everything
– Rumi

Congratulations! If you have made it this far, you are indeed committed to the journey and have arrived at the next checkpoint and challenge. Isn't that what success means in any endeavor? Each victory invites the next opportunity. We have passed the midpoint and are reaching higher elevations of love. Let's explore what it means to raise the bar and heighten your standards even more. Elevate yourself and your relationships to a place of confidence, joy, and gratitude.

In this section, we will be asking you to cross a few life-altering bridges. A bridge truly elevates and allows your passage across something previously impossible. Crossing bridges is a huge part of stepping up and over the obstacles required to reach the destination of beloved love waiting on the other side. You have a choice in how to approach these bridges. You can be hunched over and trembling in fear on a high narrow bridge, or, with shoulders squared, you can be looking straight ahead at the other side with nothing but confidence. You and your partner are both worth elevating to a more sophisticated and advanced level. You feel the potential for growth pushing behind your back. Now it is time to show yourself that you can bravely cross that bridge to have a visionary life and a transcendent love.

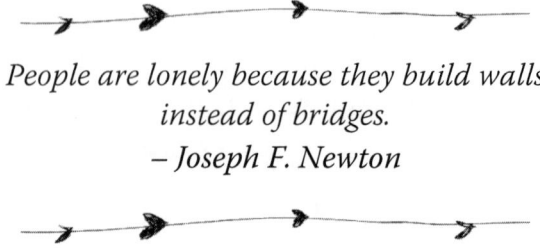

People are lonely because they build walls instead of bridges.
– Joseph F. Newton

A bridge is a transitional moment in life that is asking you to do something hard, something you are not sure you can do. To literally cross from one reality to another. It may be emotionally painful, and the outcome may be uncertain. There is risk involved and there may be questionable consequences on the other side. Yet you must go anyway. Remember the hero's journey? This is that moment. The call to adventure is like crossing a bridge, and it can be terrifying, but also euphoric.

It is the only way to elevate your life to the places you know you must go. Crossing a bridge means leaving behind who you once were in order to become who you are meant to be. You are leaving the side that is familiar, and arriving on the banks of the exotic unknown. In order to conquer the widest chasms and raging rivers of life, to elevate our understanding of who we are and what we are made of, we have to cross some scary bridges. We have to make some tricky and controversial decisions about the precariousness below. Which bridges do we avoid and which do we cross?

Reflection
Can you think of a huge transition in your life recently that felt like crossing a bridge?

Moments of change, transition, or tough decisions feel very much like being suspended on a swaying rickety footbridge with loose wooden steps. In those moments, even if you have a supportive partner (and even if you don't) the only one who can take the next step is you.

What if you take that step and the bridge breaks loose? What if you fail and fall? Being courageous goes hand in hand with fear, doubt, and also force of will. There is no other way to go, only forward, facing fear and doubt one rickety step at a time. Who are you meant to become?

Here's a little secret: when you know you are truly on your path, there is really no way to misstep. You know this is true. You have felt it before. Those moments when you absolutely know what you have to do, and a force beyond your understanding carries you to the other side. This bridge you have chosen represents the path to the best version of you. This is what it means to be fully alive. Having the will and courage to take the next step means you are committed, no matter what; somehow, some way, you will find your way across.

There is a rush of confidence and clarity when you are certain you are traversing the precise bridge on which you are meant to be. That moment when you know it is time to go, time to stay or time to make a serious change. Whatever you are afraid of, there is no stopping now. Your passage to higher love is waiting. Your future self is waiting. Your partner is waiting.

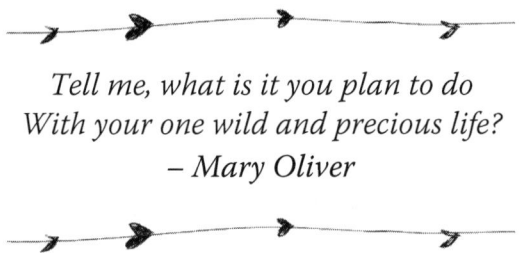

Tell me, what is it you plan to do
With your one wild and precious life?
– Mary Oliver

If you are fortunate enough to be walking across a bridge gripping a beloved's hand, the next steps might not be so frightening. But one thing is for sure, alone or together, it becomes a thrilling adventure to conquer one bridge and then the next. The scenery is exquisite when you get over your fears.

Plenty of people will want you to skip the adventure and stay home; be like everyone else. But you know that will never do. Beloveds refuse to heed the status quo. The everyday humming noise of life is not interesting to them. They require orchestras of potent experience in order to grow. Now it is time for you to learn from your past mistakes, release what no longer serves you and climb higher.

There is nothing more satisfying than taking that next step of destiny. Your self-confidence surges and you feel intuitively connected to your body and your will. Elevating in love is all about rising in esteem, clarity, and confidence. You both are committed to each other's growth. This is certain. With this knowing, you are free to face the bridges you must cross yourself. Don't worry, beloveds always wait for each other right there on the other side. Celebrate! Rejoice and watch one another grow.

Rising up to this new love may require you to do some things that seem scary. Bridges of being more vulnerable with yourself and with each other. Changing unhealthy habits. Striving for a new job or a brilliant new business idea. Saying you are sorry and meaning it. Becoming a parent. Losing a parent. Fighting a serious illness. Once you begin to address them, to cross them, these moments or transitions feel much less scary. You have to take that first step to make sure that the bridge holds, and then each next step builds confidence.

Elevating in love may mean crossing bridges of your past and leaving them behind. It's okay. Only after you have traversed the spans which no longer serve you is it possible to start designing new structures that will support your path towards Becoming Beloveds.

Reflection

We all have experienced broken hearts and difficult relationships that required us to cross scary bridges. What is the single gift you gained from crossing that bridge?

Maslow defined the word esteem as "prestige and the feeling of accomplishment." He further clarified this tier into two categories. Lower-level esteem is defined by a need for respect from others. It includes a yearning or desire for status, recognition and attention. Higher-level esteem is the desire for strength, competence, mastery, self-confidence, independence, and freedom.

When advancing through the beloved relationship hierarchy, we will be referring to the higher level of esteem that exists within a relationship. We call it "couple esteem." This can be thought of as the ability to share success, accomplishment, and value within the relationship. Individual and couple esteem are both necessary components to building belovedness in higher love.

Couple esteem is the strength of the space between the two of you. It requires attention to the same qualities of higher-level individual esteem. You will find your relationship flourishing when it is filled with strength, competence, and mastery.

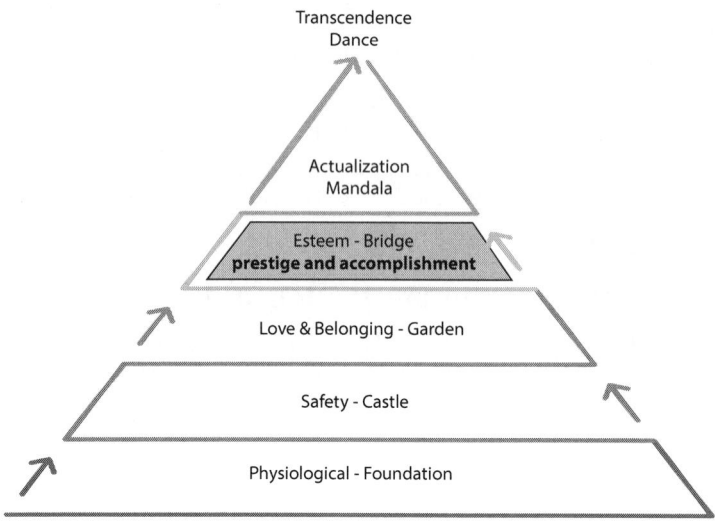

Beloved couples have something unique about the way they engage with each other that builds esteem. They are kind to each other and support each other individually, but they also place great value on the relationship itself. They speak often about their partnership and tend to the evolution of their coupling in the form of shared projects, work, community engagement, or other mission-related efforts.

Prestige is different from esteem. Prestige is more about how you let the outside world define you. There will always be those who help you to feel good about yourself, and those who want you to feel bad by comparison. Esteem comes from the inside.

Rather than having external things like prestige become a goal that ultimately only serves a superficial ego, elevate your esteem through a focus on personal strength, competence, mastery, independence, and freedom. Those are the qualities that come from the soul. Living in high esteem is not egoic, rather it allows you to project your energy more clearly. It will help you to find your perfect mate, who wants to see you as your highest self.

The most stable and therefore the most healthy self-esteem is based on deserved respect from others.
– Abraham Maslow

John Bradshaw, who was a relationship counselor and author of six best-selling books on the subject of self-esteem, was considered by his peers to be one of the most influential writers on emotional health in the twentieth century. He wrote, "We need at least one significant other who verifies our sense of worth." In a conscious relationship, beloveds reflect their partner's self-worth consistently, kindly and without any judgment. They understand the power of verifying how hard those scary bridges are to cross. They are the first ones to cheer and applaud the other's crossings and accomplishments. Building each other's self-esteem is organic, instinctive, and a source of pride.

Building couple-esteem offers an entirely new and very special bridge to cross together. Think of the possibilities! Both of you will cross the bridge at the same time and build the very soul of your relationship. This journey begins on what we call the "solid ground of respect." It is the only way you can successfully cross the bridge to your shared and solid future as beloveds.

The first suspended step in this relationship bridge is what we call "mastering autonomy," where each partner must solidify their individual sense of esteem and worth.

From there, and with growing confidence, you progress through the precarious middle portion called "meeting in the middle." You both will encounter individual diversions in your journey for rarely are we on the same step at the exact same time.

When you are sure you are never going to make it, "appreciation and gratitude" offer the last push you need to keep going.

Finally, with a triumphant final leap, you both will jump to the other side, and a fantastic moment of "celebrating bridges crossed."

Let's take a closer look at this bridge and the critical steps that bring you and your partner to an elevated and much higher understanding of what partnership can mean.

The Solid Ground of Respect

The only way to gain passage over this bridge to higher love is launching from the solid ground of respect for yourself and your partner. Respect is a feeling of deep admiration for someone or something elicited by abilities, qualities, or achievements. Each of you has to respectfully make these crossings in your own way and in your own time. Sometimes you do it together, sometimes solo, but respect is always the solid ground you can rely on.

Admiration or affirmation are respectful gifts that we can give to each other after an accomplishment of any kind and it will always strengthen the relationship. Unfortunately, when our partner crosses a major bridge, we do not always greet their achievements with admiring words and welcoming arms. Burdened by personal insecurities, it can be tempting to measure your partner's abilities against your own and become resentful, judgmental, or critical. "How come he got there so much faster?" or "She has no idea what I have on my plate..." This is a very effective way to sabotage your shared journey.

For example, you come home late from work, still elated at being offered a promotion. You forgot to call during the intensity of the negotiations. Walking in the door you are bursting with accomplishment and excitement and love for your spouse, but you are met with crossed arms and tight lips. The moment is gone. Crossing that bridge of achievement is greeted with, "Why are you so late?"

Esteem is a foundational dynamic of a good relationship, in that you cannot fully respect another's achievements or abilities unless a certain level of self-esteem is in place. A lack of respect for self and others will tumble any couple backwards into the lower levels of the relationship hierarchy, or end it altogether.

Couple-esteem requires mutual respect and admiration for each other. It requires doing personal work. Conscious couples are secure in their own competencies, thoughts and opinions. They are not afraid to voice a viewpoint contrary to their partner's. They are not afraid to disagree because there is a fundamental sense of respect between them. It is never about right and wrong, but calmly sorting through emotions and perspectives.

The beginning of love is to let those we love be perfectly themselves, and not to twist them to fit our own image. Otherwise we love only the reflection of ourselves we find in them.
— *Thomas Merton*

If a solid level of respect is not in place when couples have differing opinions, things get hurtful. Rather than thinking, "why are they being such a stubborn jerk about this?" Conscious couples ask questions like, "Why is my partner feeling so strongly about this, is it scraping an old wound? Are they afraid of something?" Thoughtful questions are the key to exploring, rather than being angered by a different point of view.

It takes both trust and vulnerability to respect each other enough to disagree, and work through challenges with benevolent mindfulness. It requires a strong sense of self and couple esteem to understand when to push or nudge each other and when to let go. A beloved must recognize the autonomy of their partner.

Mastering Autonomy

Autonomy is the ability to make your own decisions without being controlled by anyone else. If you find yourself saying, "I got this" or "Please let me do this," in your relationship, you are identifying the bridges you must cross alone, in a good way. You are voicing your need to exercise personal autonomy to make decisions or take a particular action. While the interdependence of having your beloved nearby is comforting, independence is necessary and vital to growth.

Building esteem and laying a foundation of accomplishment requires that each partner is able to act on their own while enjoying the full support of the other. Autonomy allows you to cross your very own new bridges.

Beloveds inspire and motivate each other's choices. Strong couples are happily entwined and understand the decisions they make individually impacts their partner and others in their shared world. They understand when to allow each other the space they need to do their own thing.

Reflection
Think about a time where you had to make a major transition on your own. Your partner could not help you. How did you grow through the process?

Meeting in the Middle

Sometimes, couples may face a "bridge to nowhere" disappointment, or a tricky challenge when both bridges are arching in different directions. The question arises: which bridge to cross? Who goes and who stays? How many times have you had disagreements in which one person wants to do one thing and the other does not? It is much easier when all of the previous steps in your growth journey are secure and in place. If you have your foundation, your castle and your garden, the path across the bridges will be easier to navigate.

There is a fine line between capitulating and giving your partner the freedom to explore and grow. That kind of loving balance is required when crossing the more challenging personal bridges. Each partner must allow the other the freedom to explore their own desires and ambitions. You need autonomy to act in accordance with your own direction and cross your bridge while remaining respectful of your relationship.

For example, moving or relocating is often a difficult decision in a relationship. Sometimes a different location makes sense for one person's career and that works for their autonomy and self-esteem, but it may be very different for the other partner. "I just got a great promotion but we'll have to move to ..." is the language that comes from one partner while "I don't want to live in..." comes from the other.

Reflection
Have you ever had a time in life when your personal direction in life clashed with your partner? How would you meet in the middle?

Partners have to make individual decisions while paying attention to how it will affect them as a pair. Crossing bridges into new territory of your personal and couple growth is a refined balancing act. Just being more aware makes it easier to cross the bridges. Talk it through. If each partner consciously pays attention to the other's need for autonomy they both grow.

When one partner overrides the other's decisions, they lessen the autonomy of their mate. It never ends well does it? They start going backwards on the bridge. Knowingly stopping a partner from pursuing their ambitions will quickly erode a relationship.

The trick is to meet in the middle. No matter where you stand on your current bridges of life, good or bad, taking the time to express appreciation for yourself, your partner, and for the journey itself makes each forward step worthwhile.

Broken couples often sabotage each other's esteem and autonomy. Their carefully constructed bridges falter and break. Eventually, the decision may come to leave all of the old bridges behind and have the courage to take a different path. A new bridge to find out who you really are. Perhaps you may attract a beloved who will happily want you to grow, evolve and cross bridges both alone and together. Settle for nothing less.

Appreciation and Gratitude

Beloved couples are not shy about how creatively and actively they appreciate each other as they cross little daily bridges or big long-term ones. At this level of esteem, both quality and quantity of appreciation apply. Couples who admire each other enjoy a soaring sense of self-esteem, and very high couple-esteem. Beloveds truly feel grateful to have their partners in their lives, and they tell them so in words, actions and deeds. The key is authenticity.

Authentic gratitude is different from appreciation, which is what happens when someone does something nice like fold the laundry or take out the trash. Authentic gratitude is intrinsic to love. There is a difference between expressing appreciation for an act of service or support, and the core gratitude you feel for the amazing existence of that someone in your life. Appreciation is a sincere "Thank You for walking the dog." Gratitude is more like a wellspring that is always there, as in "I don't know what I would do without you."

Both are important and everyone could use a little practice. Make an effort to be appreciative of your partner. There are many things couples do for each other every day that is easy to let go unnoticed. Notice. Thank your partner for remembering to pick up the right brand of shampoo or for grabbing the mail or remembering you needed eggs. Tell them. Appreciate the little things.

Practice gratitude. Reflect on what a gift it is to be in love at all, to have a wonderful someone to share your days and dreams with. Life is sweeter. Notice. Feel it. Take it in. Gratitude is one of the highest emotions we are capable of. It bubbles up inside of you, nourishes you, and expresses outward without effort.

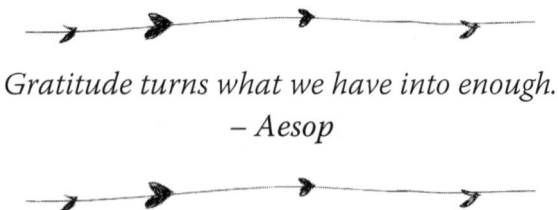

Gratitude turns what we have into enough.
– Aesop

Let's face it, life can be hard. We always remember the criticisms more than the praise. We beat ourselves up. Try not to do that. Appreciate yourself and find gratitude even in the clouds of life. The sun always comes out again. And sometimes your partner has to do something hard. They have to make decisions that they are nervous about. There is a bridge to cross, and they are scared to take the first step. This is a wonderful time to be a beloved.

Trust that they can do it and demonstrate that by not telling them what to do or not do or how to do it. Let them navigate the bridge and be there waiting for them on the other side. Show your appreciation for their grit, courage and tenacity. Find gratitude for what you share together. It makes it oh-so-much-easier to take a risk and try something new.

Reflection
How do you recognize or appreciate your partner? Do you have a practice of reflecting on what you are grateful for in your life?

Celebrating Bridges Crossed

One of the beautiful impulses of feeling deep gratitude in beloved love is a desire to show the world how important and vital your partner is in your life. It reflects a unique acceptance of your partner with all of their wonderful imperfections and a delight in their uniqueness.

It's different from unconditional love, it is instead unconditional acceptance. Beloveds flow past the dissimilarities between them; they don't see differences as incompatibilities or irritations, but as qualities they admire, respect, and learn from. Beloveds develop a deep understanding and appreciation for the entirety of their partners as individuals. They realize how much deeper and better their lives are because their partners are there with them. And they express that gratitude often.

Celebrating your partner's success at the moment they cross a personal bridge is pure joy on both sides. It is amazing to achieve and elevate to another level of skill and competence and it is wonderful to be recognized. The elation of triumph is so much better when it is shared by those we care about.

Building self-esteem means feeling settled in your established abilities and being willing to ride a learning curve to grow new competencies. It is about being curious and open. Be sure to extend the same courtesy to your partner. Recognize their genius on a regular basis, and offer encouragement when they need to forge ahead and gain new skills.

There is nothing more gratifying than that profound moment when one partner recognizes and sees the other's brilliance and can fully absorb it. We are not talking about being your partner's loudest cheerleader, but more about genuine quiet admiration when your partner has accomplished something that is important to them.

Renowned therapist Esther Perel writes about how individuals are most drawn to their partners when they witness them as a separate person doing something competently. Watching your love from a distance when they are in their "zone of genius" arouses attraction and connection. Love grows when one partner experiences the other in their most brilliant moments, big and small. When you love someone, and see them in their greatness, then love, passion, and desire are heightened.

Love rests on two pillars: surrender and autonomy.
Our need for togetherness exists alongside
our need for separateness.
– Esther Perel

Couple-esteem flourishes when those moments you recognize the brilliance of your partner are expressed. If you see it, say it! Tell your partner they are super-sexy when they buzz around the room in a rumpled tee shirt and then whip up a fantastic three course brunch with ingredients you didn't know were in the house. Praise them when they employ their hilarious wit and antics to coerce the cranky toddler to take a bath. Don't hold back when you see your partner doing something awesome. Tell them. Then bask in the resulting light of love and appreciation.

Enjoy the adrenaline ride of crossing big scary bridges and building deep esteem in your relationship as a result. After all, couple esteem and beloved love is truly a living and breathing entity that exists between you. If you only take time to praise your relationship once a year by signing your name on a store-bought Valentine's Day card, get more creative. Learn to surf together. Go skydiving, try roasted crickets! Take risks, gain skills, try something adventurous, and practice actively growing - just like you are doing right now.

Elevate in Esteem by Leaving Bridges Behind

Have you ever had to make a significant and tough decision to cut someone out of your life? Whether it is a lover, friend, co-worker, or family member it is painful. It feels like burning a bridge. This is not easy, yet it is necessary to growth. Maybe there have been times when you have had to narrow a bridge of connection with someone who is just dragging you down. Conversely, perhaps you actively want to build bridges towards those whom you admire or just love being around.

Part of maturing and elevating in love requires learning how to turn away from the bridges that no longer serve you. You must also figure out how to build bridges towards destinations that make you a better person. Elevating to your highest potential and becoming a beloved to another means that you rise up to be the best version of you. Are you still going out drinking with your college buddies while your partner waits for you at home and goes to bed alone? Maybe that is a bridge that needs to be left in the past. Being social is fine, but is this a part of your life that you really need and is it serving your higher growth?

On the flip side, have you given up many of your outside friendships to focus solely on your partner? Have you turned away from outside bridges and are feeling isolated? That's not good either. Assessing your personal circles and social patterns is helpful in building your own sense of growth and it is healthy for your relationship. We need good friends in our lives. We need new challenges. It builds our esteem in special ways and enhances our relationships with our partners.

In his landmark book *Vital Friends,* Tom Rath has shown, through Gallup Poll surveys, that having just three truly close friends – even if they are not physically close to you – can extend your life by up to seven years.

Reflection
Take a moment to review your social circles. Are there too many taking you away from personal goals? Are there too few leaving you feeling isolated? Do they support your relationship?

Take some time to examine your life and determine if there are social or friend bridges that need to be abandoned for now. Do the same as a duo. Are there couples that make you feel less than great? Let them drift away for now. Are there other couples you both really enjoy being around who are fun, interesting and positive? Build bridges in that direction.

Turn away from the people and bridges that no longer serve you. Build access to where you want to be. Jim Rohn, a well-known motivational speaker, has brilliantly said that "You are the average of the five people you spend the most time with." Choose wisely.

In matters of soul, a well-conceived ritual act, well-chosen words, an inspired gesture, a symbolic gift, even a tone of voice can achieve the desired effect. Often a very small gesture will have great consequences, this is one of the traditional rules of magic.

-Thomas Moore

Build Beloved Habits

One of the most potent and powerful tools to elevate love is to develop what we call "Beloved Habits," as a natural part of everyday life. Let's explore. Every couple has routines or habits that bolster esteem and build the relationship or ignore it or even bring it down. Little patterns or behaviors like seeing the glass half empty, complaining instead of complementing, erupting in anger over a little thing, can become negative habits, and it makes it harder to be romantic, joyful, creative or open-hearted.

Building esteem requires paying attention to the positive aspects of your relationship to flourish. Dr. Barbara Fredrickson, who developed the idea of "micro-moments" we mentioned earlier, created something called the "positivity ratio." Fredrickson discovered that experiencing three positive emotions like joy, gratitude, or optimism is required to counter one negative emotional experience of anger, fear, stress or shame. Eighty percent of Americans fall short of this three-to-one ratio in order to flourish in life.

It is sometimes easier to remember the criticism over the compliments, but if it takes three positive moments to counter that one negative one, why wouldn't you just forget the negative and focus on the positive? When our moods are positive three times more than they are negative, we reach a tipping point where we experience an "upward spiral" of positivity. Everything gets better.

By focusing on creating a three-to-one ratio of positive emotions versus negative ones as a couple, your lives will be more optimistic, inspired, joyful, and just plain happier.

Building and elevating esteem means recognizing your beloved each day and expressing moments of positivity out loud. Don't keep your compliments and praise to yourself! Build up couple-esteem by offering dollops of sincere appreciation regularly. Be generous in sharing your favorite memories together. Take notice of the milestones each of you have achieved and the combined goals you have accomplished.

Paper cuts and lightning bolts are negative habits that are hazardous to your relationship. Both of these belittle your partner and destabilize the bridge towards higher love.

Instead, utilize this positivity ratio to inspire more shared moments together and more time connecting in-between the moments of the day. Putting a sweet little note in their lunch is an example of an in-between moment. Showing up to have lunch in the park as a surprise is an example of a shared moment.

Appreciate the wonderful gift of the love you share and build positive connection habits with your beloved. It sounds simple enough, but new habits require change and an investment of energy before they become second nature.

Just like when we start a new diet or a new routine at the gym, our lazy minds will protest any new habit. The brain hates investing the extra energy to do something new. "Why do we have to connect all the time?" The brain will complain. "They already know I love them... this stuff is lame. I'm not doing this."

But if you are willing to invest literally two extra minutes a day, you will discover that beloved habits can be the planks and ropes that you use to fortify your relationship bridge. Start new habits with in-between moments of your day. Notice when you are taking a break during your routine for lunch or a transition during the day that you may fill with podcasts or social media.

These are perfect moments to practice beloved habits and reach out to your partner. Be creative. Send a little text with cute emojis or snap a picture of a blooming flower or send their favorite love song. It takes seconds of your time. Soften your voice on the phone. Rather than being overbearing or demanding, it is simply being thoughtful, surprising and sweetly present. And it is enchanting to receive.

There are so many moments in our day when we forget to enjoy the ones we love. Sometimes the daily stressors of life become so habitual we kind of forget to live. Don't do that. Build beloved habits between the moments of your day. Create more shared moments. Soon it will become second nature.

When you find yourself with the Beloved
Embracing for one breath
In the moment, you will find your true destiny,
Alas, don't spoil this precious moment
Moments like this are very, very rare.
— Shahram Shiva

CHAPTER 6

REFLECT LOVE ~ THE MANDALA

A human being evolves when it dares to look within.
- Alberto Jose Varella

Often, we believe that the only time we can reflect is by going on a retreat or somehow separating ourselves from the world. On the contrary, ten minutes spent journaling or meditating can be very effective. Maybe you prefer to do your inner reflections while on a brisk walk in the woods or at the beach. Our mind only requires a few fresh and spacious moments to soar freely and whisper that which we most need to hear.

Your next step will entail a reflective journey that explores the inward and outward edges of who you are, and who you have become.

Before we begin, take a moment to look back at the cumulative steps of your journey in life. Contemplate and celebrate the path you have traveled to reach where you are today. Think about all of the ups and downs, successes and losses, loves and heartbreaks that have led you to right here, to right now, holding this book.

You have crossed those many bridges and you have arrived here, in a new world. Your foundation is secure. Your castle is fortified, and your garden is blooming.

You are reaching the highest heights of self and couple development. As you look around at this new vista of conscious possibility, the view is lovely. The air here is sweet, the light dappled and golden. Enjoy the view in its entirety - you earned it.

In Maslow's language we are treading on the hallowed ground of self-actualization. You may feel that your journey to wholeness is complete, and indeed we are nearly there.

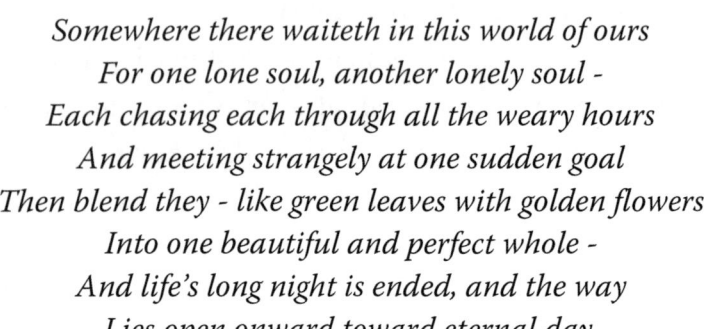

Somewhere there waiteth in this world of ours
For one lone soul, another lonely soul -
Each chasing each through all the weary hours
And meeting strangely at one sudden goal
Then blend they - like green leaves with golden flowers
Into one beautiful and perfect whole -
And life's long night is ended, and the way
Lies open onward toward eternal day.
- Sir Edwin Arnold

Wholeness. What a beautiful word. It feels settled. Satiated. When one thinks of being self-actualized, it is the sensation of being complete. It is only from this place that your relationship can also ascend into the wholeness of conscious love, the ultimate realm of the beloved. Wholeness is not reliant upon another; it is only through reaching a state of personal balance that the upper limits of love can be reached.

Reflection
Think about a moment in your life when you felt lifted to a higher place. One of those moments of sensing wholeness with yourself and the Universe. What was that moment like?

Remember our simple talisman? *Love is Easy + Love is all.* At the beginning of this journey, that talisman gave you strength and courage for the path ahead. Now that you have concluded this phase of your personal journey, your talisman might be richer, and more complex. It might be harder to fit into your pocket.

Imagine yourself and your relationship as a work of art or a living meditation, a mandala. Mandalas are sacred tools and talismans used to reflect self and spiritual development, and a perfect tool for beloveds.

The word Mandala means 'sacred circle' and is derived from the word "mandra" meaning 'container of essence'. This circle is said to represent wholeness, health, connection, harmony, and the cycle of life. It is also said to symbolize being one with life, going with the flow and reflecting inward. Creating a mandala is relaxing and contemplative and is a wonderful tool for self-reflection. Buddhist monks create stunningly intricate and ephemeral mandalas out of colored sand. You can use any materials you like, the important thing is the thought process, not the product.

Creating a mandala is truly a drawing of your inner world at any given moment and has a calming and focusing effect. It is a visual meditation that you build intuitively in layers. The result is a map of personal symbols that have meaning to you as a reflection of your evolving Self. A mandala is an emblem of life and the wholeness of the person creating it.

I sketched every morning in a notebook a small circular mandala which corresponded to my inner situation at the time. Only gradually did I discover what a mandala really is... the Self, the wholeness of the personality.
– *Carl Jung*

Carl Jung, the notable Swiss psychotherapist and psychiatrist who founded analytic psychology, was noted for his concept of individuation as a central process of human development. For Jung, the process of individuation was one that encompassed all aspects of the human being including philosophical, mystical, and spiritual. Jung is credited for bringing mandalas to the western world, and had his patients create them.

Jung was deeply influenced by the insights he found in mandalas, and spent years drawing and creating his own almost daily that were eventually published in his epic *Red Book*. It became the core of his work, represented by literally hundreds of mandalas of his and other patients. He felt they expressed both psychological and spiritual health.

Reflection
Take a moment to sketch your mandala. Maybe it is an intricate geometric circle or a colorful map. Think about the design, colors and symbols you are drawn to. What does your mandala represent at this moment in time?

Here is an example of a traditional Tibetan mandala. It is common to simply gaze upon them, allowing the eyes to eventually soften while concentrating on the image, and allowing it to absorb your attention. Often, the shapes, patterns and colors begin to work upon the unconscious. As the mind begins to "fall into the mandala" many experience a feeling of lightness, and an increase in intuitive thoughts, inner peace, and higher awareness. Give it a try.

Jung believed mandalas were archetypal forms representing the Self, or total personality, and they represent a striving for completion, balance, and unity as "archetypes of wholeness". Jung discovered that dreaming about or creating mandalas is a natural part of the individuation process in finding the Self as a representation of the unified psyche. He thought of the integration and fulfillment of this archetype into one's life as self-actualization.

Maslow incorporated the idea of self-actualization into his own work and defined the term as the growth of an individual toward fulfillment of their highest needs, those most advanced concepts and big questions like the meaning of life.

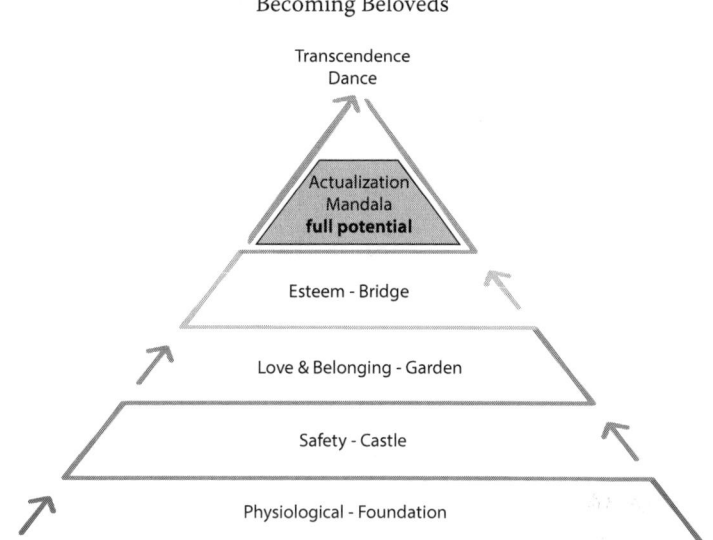

As we follow the flow of Maslow's Hierarchy of Needs applied to the evolution of love, we have reached the top level. Self-actualization is the drive to become the best version of yourself. It is more of a reflective process rather than having a transcendental experience.

Self-actualization could be found by pursuing a very concrete goal like using your athletic talents to be the best in a given sport, being the best listener in the room, or the most amazing parent you know how to be. The goal is to become everything you are capable of becoming, realizing your highest potential and always seeking growth.

This tendency might be phrased as the desire to become more and more what one is, to become everything that one is capable of becoming.
- Abraham Maslow

Self-actualization takes significant thought and effort to achieve. For couples, it requires drive and intention times two. Both you and your partner must be willing to do the work to attain this level of the journey. If you are both striving to reach this peak, then you can evolve together and travel the next steps arm in arm.

Things are looking pretty magnificent up here at the top. You are now at a place that feels solid, engaged and flourishing. Your relationship is connected, powerful, and maybe a little bit enchanted. Fantastic! Don't stop now! Let's keep going.

This stage is all about evolution. Your sense of self is solid and strong, and your relationship has a vibrant and fluidly positive quality. Taking personal self-actualization and entwining it with your partner's creates a mandala of love. As each person becomes whole in and of themselves, the relationship becomes complete. The mandala is balanced and harmonized. Without each party achieving a certain level of their own self-actualization, an evolved relationship is hard to achieve. Both parties must climb this stage together to be in service to each other and to the world.

Maslow noticed that while most all of us are capable of reaching this level, many of us do not succeed. Many couples have the capacity to reach an expanded relationship yet settle for less. Maslow noted several characteristics of self-actualized people, including experiencing life like a joyful child, trying new things, not caring about what other people think of you, and avoiding pretense.

Additionally, Maslow studied 18 people he felt were some of our most gifted self-actualized role models, including Albert Einstein, Eleanor Roosevelt and Mother Theresa. He identified fifteen common characteristics, including accepting themselves and others for who they are, an unusual sense of humor, high creativity, concern for the welfare of others, strong moral ethics, spontaneity, a need for privacy, and a deep appreciation for basic life experiences.

Reflection
Which of these characteristics stand out to you as being critical to a beloved relationship? How can you build more of them within yourself and with a partner?

While we are not advocating these characteristics as a checklist for you or your partner, there is a lot that can be translated into conscious love. Go back through the list and look at it from the perspective of being a student of higher love and from the lens of couple actualization.

Individuals and couples who have investigated the lower levels of the pyramid are now ready to explore two nuanced characteristics that have a significant impact on their individual and couple actualization. These are the qualities of sovereignty and resilience.

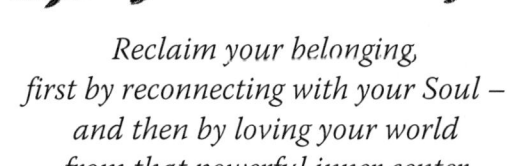

Reclaim your belonging,
first by reconnecting with your Soul –
and then by loving your world
from that powerful inner center
of love, sovereignty and wholeness.
– Hiro Boya

Sovereignty does not seem like a word that would appear in the upper echelons of a relationship, but it is an important dynamic to understand. Many think of the word sovereignty as something political, like declaring independence from another country. So, what does it mean for beloved couples to have sovereignty together? Within a relationship think of it as personal space and the understanding that each individual has a right to their own domains in multiple dimensions of life. It is about freedom.

Beloveds don't hover over each other or constantly insert their opinions, preferences, and habits. Forcing yourself into someone else's sovereignty is an invasion of privacy and respect. This is not how a loving relationship grows.

Conscious individuals and couples recognize that each partner needs to have their own domains in which to make decisions, grow, and develop. Sovereignty is being able to make individual decisions that do not specifically impact the intimate relationship, such as professional choices, familial relations, personal health, spiritual pursuits, or personal hobbies. Having someone invade your personal space or try to impact these choices feels like having your sovereignty invaded.

Recognizing where and when your personal space ends and your partner's personal space begins is what sovereignty means in a relationship. Understanding the borders around each partner and around a couple involves actively discussing and agreeing on where these boundaries are. Sovereignty can be effortless, but sometimes these discussions can be so subtle that it can be difficult to know if and when we are in each other's space, so tread carefully.

Reflection
In what areas of life do you feel the need for sovereignty? What happens if it conflicts with someone you are in a relationship with?

For example, if one partner struggles with an aging parent and has to be deliberate with their adult siblings about long-term care, it is that partner, and their siblings' sovereign domain to make those decisions. The boundaries around those decisions sit squarely with the partner and siblings whose parent needs attention. Of course, the other partner can be there as a sounding board and source of support. However, interfering in the process and outcomes would violate that partner's sovereignty.

Let's look at sovereignty in personal health. Each partner in the relationship has to take ownership over their own physical fitness. One partner may be in the gym six days a week, the other may be an occasional walk-around-the-block kind of person. One partner might be crazy for carbs, and the other may be leaning towards keto.

Each has sovereignty to make choices regarding what their body wants and needs. One does not have to automatically eat the same special diet or do the same workout routine.

When the borders of each partner's sovereignty are clear and boundaries have been communicated, a beloved relationship arises like a breath of fresh air. Beloveds accept each other's individuality and choices. They become true partners and can explore new ideas, joys, fears, triumphs and frustrations together.

Sovereignty is about standing at your partner's side and not trying to intervene, interject, or repair. Know that your partner can let you be who you are, and that you can do the same for them. Respecting your partner's sovereignty reflects the deeper soul of a relationship.

When you love with no conditions, you the human and you the God align with the Spirit of Life moving through you. Life becomes the expression of the beauty of the Spirit. Life is nothing but a dream and if you create your life with Love, your dream becomes a masterpiece of art.
-Don Miguel Ruiz

Resilience is the ability to adapt to and recover from change or misfortune. It means bouncing back from difficult and challenging experiences. Resilience grows with time and experience. Understanding what builds resilience in love is important to furthering our mental, emotional and spiritual health as a conscious couple.

Paula Davis-Laack, author of the book *STRONG: Stress Relief Strategies When You're Short On Time*, defines resilience as "the capacity for stress-related growth" and states that resilience is required on pretty much a daily basis. As we get older and have more experience with stress, we can feel more optimistic because we understand our capacity for resilience.

Mature relationships also build confidence and elasticity as couples learn to repair and heal after setbacks and adversity. Strong partners protect and shield each other from unnecessary stress or negativity. They have empathy for each other and are able to reframe and rethink tough situations. Over time this reinforces the foundation of any relationship, knowing you are more resilient with your partner than on your own. One of the gifts of being with a beloved is the deep comfort that comes from your shared resilience.

Let's reflect how this quality of resilience flows upward through each of the levels on our relationship hierarchy of needs.

Building your solid foundation allows you the ability to retreat to the comfort of your castle or home without worry or judgment. The strong security of physical and emotional safety is soul-nourishing and engenders confidence.

Even if you are not sure what you need in the moment, being brave enough to voice your doubt builds resilience. Exercise your autonomy; stand up for yourself, speak your truth, and recognize when you need to ask for support or space. Utilize your partner and your tribe for support. In return, giving to someone in distress is a powerful bonding gesture, and being able to receive in kind reflects high esteem.

Reflection
How has life taught you resilience? How can you foster that resilient strength more actively?

Resilience is strengthened by sovereignty. No matter the adversity you are facing, you have the ability to make choices for yourself. You get to decide. If you get knocked down it is just that, you got knocked down. You have the power and the will to stand back up and try again, or walk away. Your highest self automatically accesses that growth mindset. You get to choose what to do, and engage on that decision.

If you have seen your partner feeling particularly vulnerable after suffering a tragedy or loss, it elicits a profound desire to engage and support them to help them find their resilience. Offering tools that build your strength as a couple can be very healing. Sometimes just being together is enough. Simply being present for your partner is what beloveds do.

Cultivating resilience as a pair builds unbreakable bonds. When there is a siege at the door, knowing you have a deep foundation, a moat surrounding your castle, an army of protectors ready, and secure quarters in which to retreat, you can weather any storm.

The Wholeness of Beloveds

Wholeness is not achieved by cutting off a portion of one's being, but by integration of the contraries.
– Carl Jung

What does it mean to think of yourself as whole? It is the integration of all the lessons you have learned and all of the bridges you have crossed. Wholeness is the realization that body and spirit are constantly renewed. It is the decision to relinquish the broken pieces of your past that no longer define or serve you and spin a gorgeous mandala that is uniquely yours.

It takes some practice to let go of our wounds. Subconsciously these injuries may have gained us sympathy and attention that we don't want to lose, but we really have to let them go. Healing can be as easy as releasing the clenched fist, liberating your wound, and allowing your palm to relax and open in your lap. To emerge as a whole human is a wonderful process. It is about letting go of your past, owning your worth, claiming your strengths and living from the Now.

Becoming a beloved to yourself is a necessary step towards becoming a beloved to another. You will need to bring yourself into the fortitude of wholeness. It does not come without work, but you've done the work. Take a look at where you are.

In life, we are often focused only on the ladder above us. We climb our way to the next rung, and are told not to look down. Now you can bravely look down. See how far you have come. Notice how strong you are, how much more you know and understand about yourself than ever before. Enjoy the view from the top. It is from this place you can come together in an entirely new form of union.

CHAPTER 7

EXPAND AND DECLARE LOVE ~ THE DANCE

Two souls are sometimes created together
and in love before they are born.
– F. Scott Fitzgerald

Think about those moments when you feel your soul surging with the divine joy of declaring your love to another: *"I love you."* Your heart races even as time seems to stand still. The noises of the outside world settle into deafening silence. There is nothing but that moment; pure, ephemeral and unforgettable at the same time.

"I love you too." And nothing is ever the same. A new dance has begun, and it feels as expansive as soaring to the stars. The shared declaration sweeps you up like a rocket and brings both of you charging into a glorious new vista of possibility. Because it is. Pure possibility. You can have any life you want. All you have to do is decide.

Sharing love with someone is the very reason we are on this planet. When you are brave enough to declare love, and dedicated enough to build a strong, connected, whole and conscious relationship, there is simply no stopping you. You are at the top. The infinity. Alpha to omega. The beginning and the end. Now it is all about savoring, rejoicing, giving back... and dancing.

Reflection
Think of a moment when you felt the purest sensation of love. How would you describe that moment?

For some couples, you may have reached this place of higher love long ago and perhaps have forgotten how powerful and magnificent it is. Maybe you used to dance, not just literally going out dancing together, you also danced intellectually, emotionally, and in sensuality. Take back that tango. Travel this journey together to Become Beloveds as a renewed dance. Let it take you deeper and higher than ever.

For some couples who are just starting on the journey of love and commitment, know that you can craft an enviable beloved love if you put in the time and invest in your evolving dance.

For those waiting for a beloved, the very effort of bringing yourself to this point gives you the ability to attract, recognize and entwine with the right partner. So, do your own dance.

For all who have arrived at the top of this marvelous journey, look around. Your foundation is firm, your castle safe and protected. Gardens are blossoming and bridges have been crossed. You have traveled the serpentine path of the mandala and returned wiser and renewed. It is glorious.

Love does not consist of gazing at each other, but in looking outward together in the same direction.
- Antoine de Saint-Exupery

This is a moment of exquisite expansion, a time to celebrate the energy of your togetherness, and a time to evolve outward. Love is a choice. Choose to renew and surrender to the depths of love again and again. Relish the moments of life that serve to expand you, your partner, and your conscious relationship.

Decide to stay connected always and to marvel in the wonder of your partner in their constantly changing humanness. Take every moment to grab her hand, to tell him you are proud of him. Become opportunists of love and seize every chance to stop everything, embrace and kiss. Be exceedingly grateful for every single second you have.

We have now arrived at the highest point of Maslow's original Hierarchy of Needs. His most popular work shows the top of the pyramid to be the level of self-actualization. However, in his later years he amended his work and added a master level: that of transcendence. This is the place where you realize there is more than just your own evolution. Here is where you look outside of yourself to the beckoning of your calling or destiny. The realm of transcendence involves finding a higher purpose, and having what are called peak experiences.

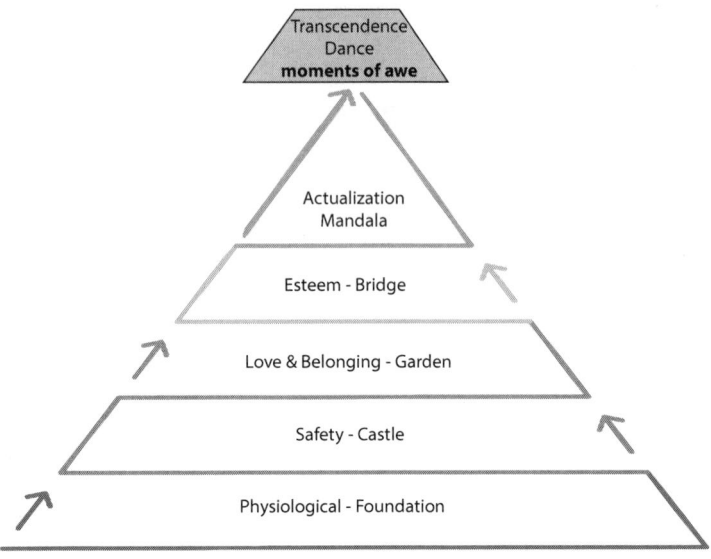

Maslow defined this level as "feelings of limitless horizons opening up to the vision, the feeling of being simultaneously more powerful and also more helpless than one ever was before, the feeling of great ecstasy wonder and awe." Sounds like love, doesn't it? Maslow said further, "the lovers come closer to forming a unit rather than two people."

Beyond everyday love, castles and pyramids, we are now at a place to experience pure expansion. We are exploring a level of growth that is ethereal and even mystical in its expression. My beloved. Your beloved. Beloved Love.

He felt now that he was not simply close to her but that
he did not know where he ended and she began.
- Leo Tolstoy

The gift of a beloved offers the possibility to experience moments of transcendence, awe and gratitude with your partner, and to become an example to others. Just by being unabashedly in love, others will smile as you saunter by hand in hand. They may become inspired watching you smile and giggle while being enraptured in some discussion at lunch.

Becoming beloveds is not just meeting your mate and enjoying a hedonistic ride. Those who arrive in this arena find that their union leads to a shared and respectful sense of purpose. There is a humility and reverence that comes from being given this special gift, and there is a desire to re-gift it in the most generous way possible. It is recognizing a higher mission.

If you have that special kind of relationship and can humbly relate to reaching this level as a couple, you have figured out how to navigate the minutia of everyday life. The skills of maintaining thoughtful, meaningful and tender habits for yourself and your partner have been mastered. You have learned how to understand and follow both your personal and shared dreams and achieved a level of wholeness that secures you and elevates you above everyday fears and issues.

Reflection
What intention do you have to make, every day moving forward to reach this peak? Think of a couple who embody this dance.

Couples who find themselves here often discover that language fails them. The emotion and experience are so profound that they are nearly impossible to put into words. That is the transcendent piece, where love is bigger than vocabulary and language, and can transport us to a place of speechless awe.

Beloveds who have reached this level demonstrate time and again a profound desire to share what they have learned. They want to expand their reach as a couple and share a purpose to give back locally or globally. It becomes sheer joy to develop projects and passions together. Love that glows inside shimmers outwards to touch others, even if the couple has no idea it is happening. It is a grand pay-it-forward type of love.

I am only the house of your beloved,

not the beloved herself:

true love is for the treasure,

not for the coffer that contains it.

The real beloved is that one who is unique,

who is your beginning and your end.

When you find that one,

you'll no longer expect anything else:

that is both the manifest and the mystery.

That one is the lord of states of feeling,

dependent on none;

month and year are slaves to that moon.

When he bids the "state,"

it does His bidding;

when that one wills, bodies become spirit.

- Rumi

Transcendence is fueled through finding individual purpose and creating shared endeavors as a beloved pair. One of the basics of discovering our individual purpose lies in understanding what we want to do or to be beyond the everyday. What is our legacy, our destiny? Those questions are the sweet little whispers of knowing that this relationship, this opportunity, or this inspiration is part of our reason for being placed on this earth. Recognition of why we are here then becomes a directive.

If an individual is going through the motions of life without a purpose, they will experience suffering, as will their work and family. Naturally their intimate relationships falter as well. Richard Leider, an award-winning writer and speaker on the subject, wrote a book called *The Purpose Manifesto*. He defined it as: "Your aim or goal. Your reason for being. Your reason for getting up in the morning. Most of us have wondered about a reason to get up in the morning, at least occasionally. The power of purpose, is about that reason: to help unlock the purpose of your life."

If you cannot identify a powerful reason to get up in the morning, your partner cannot find or unlock it for you. The power of reaching transcendence is the ability to see beyond our egoic efforts and to identify ways of making an impact on the world around us.

Purpose may be found in art, business, charity, volunteerism, or civic engagement; anything that stirs your passion and lifts you above yourself. There is a perfectly precise word in Japanese that captures this sense of purpose: Ikigai.

Pronounced "eye-key-guy," it means "a reason for being" and represents the source of value in one's life or the things that make one's existence feel worthwhile. It is basically the reason you get out of bed in the morning, although it sounds more elegant in Japanese.

When you are living your Ikigai, you are radiating all of your best qualities. Your essence takes the lead. Those who are actively searching for transcendence find purpose in many things. It need not be grandiose. Ikigai may be found in simple tasks of tending a garden or taking care of a dear friend during a convalescence.

Beloveds find Ikigai both in their individual calling and in their shared purpose together. Higher love is meant to be demonstrated and shared; it is not just about celebrating your love alone. It is about offering it to others who are in need of the surplus you have.

Bringing a conscious sense of purpose to your life as a couple provides the nourishment and encouragement a relationship needs to grow. Re-examine daily tasks or mundane projects and infuse them with imagination, creativity and purpose.

For small creatures such as we,
the vastness is bearable only through love.
– Carl Sagan

A profound gift of living your purpose is in experiencing moments when you can be aware of a tiny detail so vast and moving that it transforms and transcends your world. Being awake to that moment overlooking the Grand Canyon at dawn, or catching the first snowflake on your tongue on a sparkling winter day. Listening to a piece of music that makes you cry and brings goosebumps of joy at the same time.

One of the best words to describe a moment of transcendence is pure awe. What is awe? Perhaps it is an experience we may think is random or comes as a rare surprise. Stumbling upon a mind-blowing sunset coupled with a full moon rising can inspire a moment of awe so powerful you have to pull over to the side of the road to take it in. However, it is possible to cultivate moments of awe by paying attention and putting yourself into a mindset to see it.

According to University of California Professor Dacher Keltner, "we feel the sublime not just during religious ritual or in communion with God, but in everyday perceptual experiences: hearing thunder, being moved by music, seeing repetitive patterns of light and dark. Awe is to be found in daily life."

Indeed, living your purpose or Ikigai is finding awe in the everyday moments. Keltner's research at the Greater Good Science Center shows that experiencing moments of awe frequently inspires us to engage in greater acts of kindness, relieves depression, and helps us to be more present.

We believe this too. When you find moments of awe in your everyday life, you will be inspired. You will bring that vibrance home to your beloved, your family, and your community. Together, create opportunities to experience awe more often in your relationship. Ditch the dull routines to find shared inspiration. Forget Netflix and watch the stars. Walk barefoot. Kiss for hours. It will infuse your relationship with an energy that becomes a wellspring. Then, with equal energy, seek out ways, big and small, to share moments of awe with others in your world. What are you waiting for? Don't live a small life. Go big!

Reflection
Take a moment to recall an experience of awe you have had in your life. What remains with you now as you think back on it?

Think about life and love as a harmonic flowing dance. A resonant and perfect blend of music and movement. What is your dance of choice? Is it a sexy salsa or an elegant waltz? Maybe hip-hop is your thing. Imagine that your world is a big boisterous dance and how magical that would feel. You have made it this far; you are now cordially invited to pirouette at the top of the pyramid!

When you meet the one
who changes the way your heart beats,
dance with them to that rhythm
for as long as the song lasts.
– Kirk Diedrich

Any kind of dance is a celebration; it opens our hearts so our spirits can run free. Dance in the kitchen, in the bathroom, at the grocery store, or while waiting for the crosswalk. Dance and declare your love whenever and wherever you can. Tell the world about your blessings and shout it from the rooftops. Declare your love over and over. Come up with new moves. We need you to lead the way.

So many people wonder, is this the person I am meant to be with forever? Is this relationship going to last? How do I know if this is my beloved? We can't answer that question for you, but if you have done the inner work, and then taken the time to review your partnership through a beloved lens, you'll know. You won't need an outside source to verify, or a therapist, or scores of friends to give you their sage advice.

Beloved relationships stand out precisely because they look and feel so deeply in sync without needing a lot of analyzing, processing, or explanation. Malcom Gladwell perfectly described this experience in his book, *Blink: The Power of Thinking Without Thinking*, "We need to respect the fact it is possible to know without knowing why we know and accept that sometimes we're better off that way."

So, if you have a beloved, live your dance and get in sync. Blink together and watch things unfold easily and effortlessly. Find your best tempo, and rhythm, and go for it. Tango with each other's temperaments, sway with each other's moods, then sashay through the triumphs and the struggles. Unexpected turns of events simply reflect a change in the beat; nothing more, nothing less. No matter what: keep dancing.

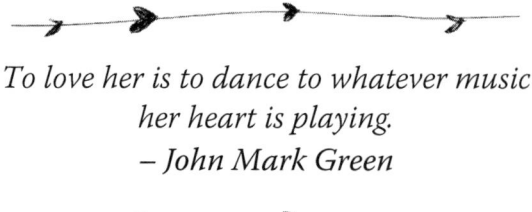

To love her is to dance to whatever music
her heart is playing.
– John Mark Green

It matters not if you are searching, waiting, dating, in a new relationship or a mature one: Love is renewable energy. In order to tap into it, this energy requires choice, intention, decision, and action. Remember,

Me + You = Us 2.0.

The Us 2.0 has all the juice and all the power.

Be Love + Be Loved = Beloveds is the ultimate dance.

Let's come together and inspire couples around the world to engage in the revelations that beloved love can offer. In little ways. In big ways. We want to see a new tribe of divine lovers and conscious couples out there redefining and demonstrating what a gift relationship can be. Our world is starving for connection, role models, and inspiration.

As a final piece of your journey with this book, create an initiation. A ritual. Write a love manifesto, a glorious mission statement about the kind of life and success you want to have. Declare becoming a student of higher love as your guide to a shared pursuit of happiness. Make yourself happy. Make each other ecstatic. Light up the sky.

Decide to follow your bliss. Dedicate your life to the pursuit of earning the gift of being a beloved to someone else. Find moments of awe, push yourself to keep exploring, to continue opening, to cultivate curiosity, to be softer, and to climb higher.

This journey always begins and ends with you. Do it for you. Scale the highest peaks, savor the rarefied air, and then return home to share the story. Let love be your endless teacher. Be an example.

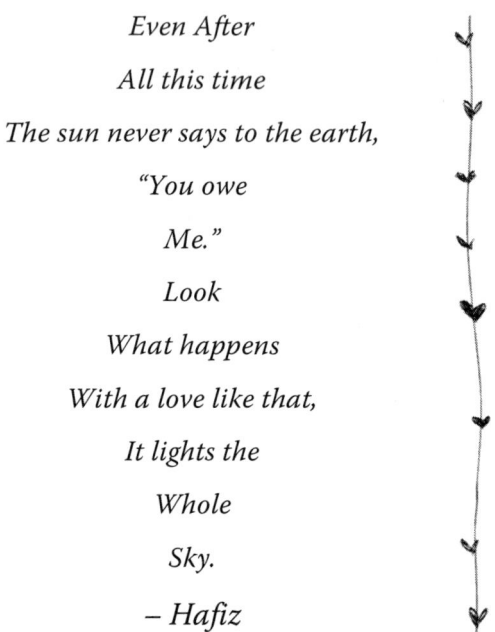

Even After

All this time

The sun never says to the earth,

"You owe

Me."

Look

What happens

With a love like that,

It lights the

Whole

Sky.

– Hafiz

In this final moment of expanding to the stars and beyond, there is an opportunity to deepen your understanding of the beloved puzzle we shared at the beginning of this book.

The meaning of beloved is to BE Love and to Be LOVED. There is a shared purpose in this mantra to give, and to receive.

As you look upward into the cosmos or down into the very reaches of your soul, there is one driving force: the heart. It is the center of the body and the center of our desires. Look at the words one more time. Say it out loud: *"BE Love."*

What does it mean to you now?

Giving love is one of the most precious aspects of being alive. BE Love by giving love all the time, as if your life depended on it, because it does. Express all that you have inside of you. Do not hold back. Share and express and demonstrate love at every opportunity. With each twist and turn of life comes a decision; give in to fear or surrender to love.

That is your purpose, your Ikigai. It will inspire transcendent awe and a connection with the Cosmos. It is an understanding that all of life is a choice and the choice is love. Give. Be Love.

And now comes the second part of the puzzle. Say it gently to yourself as if you were your very own lover: *"Be LOVED."*

What does it mean to you now?

Receive love because you deserve it, precisely as you are. There is no need for pretense, accomplishment or accolade. You are loved.

Allow your partner to love you. In all of their perfect and imperfect ways. The acts of love do not matter. Your heart can easily surmount the little missteps and mistakes in order to connect soul to soul. You are loved. Your partner loves you. If you have a beloved, they want nothing more than to experience the essence of you and be enchanted by it again and again. There is nothing more awe-inspiring than love. True love. Deep love. Expressed love. Allow yourself to merge your heart with your beloved. Let it sink in that you are loved. Someone adores you and you return the feeling. Love is everywhere, but deep transcendent love is rare indeed, a precious jewel never to be taken for granted.

Beloved.

What does it mean to you now?

The puzzle embedded in the cosmos. A word evoked for thousands of years. A mystery. A longing. A gift. A journey. Take it. Claim it. Run with it. Do something magical. Be exceptional people and extraordinary lovers of the universe.

You know you're in love when you can't fall asleep
because reality is finally better than your dreams.
– Theodor Seuss Geisel (Dr. Seuss)

And now, we leave you with the original poem that accompanied us on our beloved journey to read one last time.

Beloved Love

That's all there is

It's all there ever will be

The entrance and the path

Earn Love

Create Love

Build Love

Nurture Love

Elevate Love

Reflect Love

Expand Love

Declare Love

BE Love

Be LOVED

Become a beloved to another

Allow another to become your beloved

Let's Begin.

ABOUT THE AUTHORS

*Kari Henley is an entrepreneur and founder of **Community Without Borders**. She is an expert in elevating audience engagement, live and online through consulting, training, hosting and strategic planning. She has a master's degree in archetypal psychology, served as a weekly contributor to the Huffington Post, appeared on local TV, **Dateline, PBS "This Emotional Life"** and contributed to the Amazon bestseller, **"Embracing Your Authentic Self."***

*Steven Cardinale is an award-winning entrepreneur, author of **Synaptic Alchemy**, and founder of **Liquid Animals**, a SAAS startup. As Founder & CEO of **CID Management**, he grew the company from startup through acquisition. With an Economics degree from UCLA and an MBA from Wharton School of Business, he is currently a writer, thought leader, startup consultant, investor and business advisor.*

Together, we conceived and birthed this beautiful little book to illustrate our own insights and process to discover a more conscious and enchanted journey of Becoming Beloveds.

ABOUT STARDUST & HONEY

Stardust & Honey is a relationship development company dedicated to exploring the depth and sweetness of love. Our mission is to inspire individuals and couples to reimagine romance, reinvent relationships and remind the world of the powerful and transcendent journey to Become Beloveds. Check out our signature experiences, monthly beloved habits and online courses.

Connect Online. Visit
www.BecomingBeloveds.com
for your unique online extras